Lean & Mean
Borland C++

Bruneau Babet

////Brady

Brady Publishing

A Division of Prentice Hall Computer Publishing
201 W. 103rd St.
Indianapolis, IN 46290

ISBN: 1-56686-134-9

Library of Congress Catalog No.: 93-075009

Printing Code: The rightmost double-digit number is the year of the book's printing; the rightmost single-digit number is the number of the book's printing. For example, 94-1 shows that the first printing of the book occurred in 1994.

97 96 95 94   4 3 2 1

Manufactured in the United States of America.

About the Author

Bruneau Babet has been with Borland International for more than three years. Before joining the ObjectWindows development team recently, he was a senior technical advisor with Borland's C++ support group.

Credits

Publisher
Rick Ranucci

Managing Editor
Kelly D. Dobbs

Product Development Specialist
Sunthar Visuvalingam

Copy Editors
JoAnna Arnott
Tim Cox
Howard Jones

Editorial Assistant
Debbie McBride

Technical Editor
Mark T. Edmead

Book Designer
Kevin Spear

Cover Designer
Jay Corpus

Imprint Manager
Scott Cook

Production Analyst
MaryBeth Wakefield

Indexer
C. A. Small

Production Team
Gary Adair, Brad Chinn, Kim Cofer, Meshell Dinn, Mark Enochs,
Stephanie Gregory, Jenny Kucera, Beth Rago, Marc Shecter, Greg Simsic,
Kris Simmons, Carol Stamile, Robert Wolf

Product Marketing Manager
Debra Kempker

Acknowledgments

Thank you Borland C++ Support Team for offering an environment rich in free-flowing ideas; I am particularly appreciative of Charlie Calvert's support. Thank you to Nan Boresson of Borland International and to Sunthar Visuvalingam of Brady Publishing for being so helpful. And most of all, thank you to my wife Odette and our small family: Calypso (Swedish Warmblood), Chamonix (Lab-Chow-Husky), and Chocolat (Shepherd-mix).

Contents

Introduction

This book is about using Borland C++ with special emphasis on the C++ implementation of Borland's compiler. As such, the bulk of the material is made up of concise descriptions of features accompanied by snippets of code illustrating their usage. In addition, tips and hints mainly describing C++ idioms that make efficient use of the language feature are included throughout the book.

For example, in Chapter 5, the novice programmer will find a concise description of the C++ new operator as a flexible method for allocating dynamic memory. Several samples illustrate the use of the operator. The section on overloading operator new to monitor memory allocation will appeal to more sophisticated users. The tip on using the placement syntax of operator new to (indirectly) call the constructor of an already constructed object illustrates a technique seldom documented.

How This Book Is Organized

The beginning chapters of this book cover the basics of the Borland C++ environment and the fundamentals of C and C++. The later chapters cover more advanced material including some recent C++ additions:

- C++ templates
- C++ exception handling

- Runtime type information

- New typecast operators

Each chapter can be read independently, although the samples may make use of material covered earlier in the book. Therefore, it's best to skip only the material with which you feel completely comfortable.

Chapter 1
Borland C++ Basics

The components of Borland C++ are primarily used to create and maintain executables and libraries. The package also includes a host of utilities that can be used separately to perform other tasks, such as inspecting a file's structure or sketching an icon. The goal of this chapter is to provide a basic introduction to the tools of Borland C++.

The first section shows you how to create executables and libraries using either the Borland C++ Integrated Development Environment (IDE) or the command line tools. The next section provides information that makes it easier for you to update existing code for Borland C++.

The C/C++ language changes and runtime library modifications from earlier versions of the compiler are discussed. This material also is useful if you plan to port code that was written for another C or C++ compiler.

This chapter does not include any tutorial about the C or C++ language. However, novice programmers and experienced coders new to the Borland C++ environment will benefit from a good understanding of the steps involved in the creation of applications and libraries using Borland C++ tools.

Using the Tools

At the heart of the Borland C++ package are the core tools: compilers, librarians, and linkers. These tools process your source code, object modules, and libraries to generate the finished product: applications.

Understanding the Role of Compilers, Librarians, and Linkers

C and C++ programs are made from source files (commonly with the .C or .CPP extensions for C and C++ source modules, respectively) and header files (with the .H extension). Figure 1.1 illustrates the steps involved and the role of compilers, librarians, and linkers in the process of building a simple application.

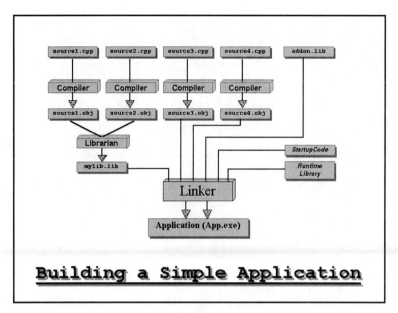

Figure 1.1. *Steps to create a simple application.*

In other words, to generate an application you do the following:

1. First, you must compile your C or C++ source file(s) to object modules. Note that header files (.H files) are not compiled; they are included by C and C++ source files.

2. Then you may combine some of the object modules into a library using a librarian.

3. Finally, you must link your object modules, libraries, and third-party libraries with the Borland C++ StartupCode and runtime library to create the final application.

The following section guides you through the steps to build a simple application using the Borland C++ IDE.

Using the Borland C++ IDE

The Borland C++ Integrated Development Environment (IDE) combines a project manager, an editor, a C/C++ compiler, a librarian, a linker, an integrated debugging facility, and more. You can create libraries and applications for DOS, Windows 16-bit, Win32s, and Windows NT using the IDE.

Tip: Windows Environments: NT, Win32, Win32s

Windows NT is a Microsoft operating system. It is available for the Intel 80386 and higher processors and includes several features, such as flat model 32-bit programming, preemptive multitasking, and security.

Win32 is the API implemented by Windows NT. It is basically an enhanced 32-bit version of the Win16 API. Win32 also refers to the primary subsystem of Windows NT.

Windows 16-bit refers to Windows v3.x and Windows for Workgroups. It is a graphical environment running on top of DOS and providing features, such as non-preemptive multitasking and data-sharing capabilities among applications.

Win16 is the API implemented by Windows 16-bit. It consists of functions to manage core system, window, and graphical objects, as well as a host of extensions including DDE, Common Dialogs, and TrueType Fonts.

Win32s is an extension that allows 32-bit Windows NT applications to run under Windows 16-bit. It is implemented via a series of DLLs and a virtual device driver. (The files are included with your copy of Borland C++.) Although Win32s allows any Win32 application to run under Windows v3.x, it implements only a subset of the Win32 API.

The terms *Win32 application* and *Windows NT application* are used interchangeably and refer to an application that runs under Windows NT or Win32s. Similarly, the terms *Win16 application* and *16-bit Windows application* are used interchangeably and refer to an application targeting Windows 3.x or Windows for Workgroups. A Win32s application is a Win32 application, which only requires the subset of the Win32 API implemented by Win32s to run properly.

Using the IDE with a Single Module

As illustrated in figure 1.1, most executables are developed using several source files. It is not uncommon, however, for utilities or small applications to be created from a single module. Following are the steps to build an application from a single source file:

1. If the source file already exists, open it by selecting Open from the File menu. Otherwise, from the File menu, choose New. Type the code in the new editor window and save the source to a file by selecting Save from the File menu. (You can use the single routine from HELLO.CPP, shown in figure 1.2, if you don't have a sample file.)

2. Activate the editor's local menu by using the right mouse button to click in the middle of the window (or by pressing Alt+F10) and select the Target Expert option (see fig. 1.2).

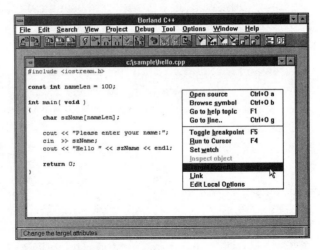

Figure 1.2. *Using the Borland C++ IDE.*

The TargetExpert dialog box appears.

3. Choose the appropriate settings for your application and select the OK button. For example, the HELLO.CPP sample can be built as a DOS standard application, a Windows 3.x (16) EasyWin application, or a Win32 Console application. Figure 1.3 illustrates the TargetExpert settings for an EasyWin application.

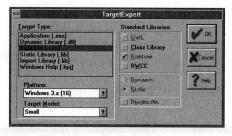

Figure 1.3. *TargetExpert settings.*

4. From the Debug menu, select Run.

The Compile Status dialog box appears while the file is compiled and linked. If there are no compiler or linker error messages, the application runs.

Projects and Multimodule Targets

When using multiple modules to create an application or library, you must create a project. A *project* is a file that contains all the information necessary to create an application or library, including the target environment, the tools settings, and the input files.

Borland C++ project files use the .IDE extension. The targets created by a project are not limited to applications and libraries. Actually, the Borland C++ IDE itself is not limited to C or C++ programs. Both the IDE and the project manager provide extensions that enable you to process arbitrary files and to generate arbitrary targets.

Figure 1.4 illustrates two C++ modules: main.cpp and greet.cpp.

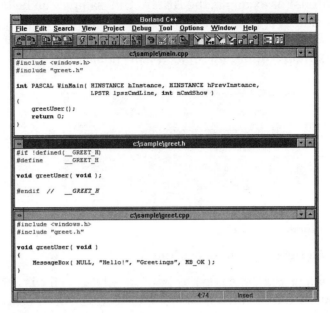

Figure 1.4. *Files of a simple program.*

The following steps show you how to create a project that builds an application from these two modules:

1. From the Project menu, select New Project.

   The New Project dialog box appears. This dialog box is an enhanced version of the TargetExpert dialog box already discussed.

2. In the New Project dialog box, you specify the name of project, the name and type of target, and the appropriate Borland C++ library settings. You can, for example, build the samples already discussed for the Windows 3.x (16) or the Win32 GUI environment. Figure 1.5 shows the settings for the Windows 3.x (16) environment.

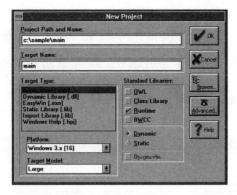

Figure 1.5. *Sample project settings.*

3. Because the program does not make use of resources or include a .DEF file, select the **A**dvanced button to further customize the project.

   The Advanced Options dialog box appears.

4. Turn off the **.rc** and **.d**ef check boxes, as shown in figure 1.6.

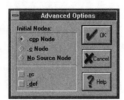

Figure 1.6. *The Advanced Options dialog box.*

5. Close the Advanced Options and New Project dialog boxes by selecting their OK buttons.

   A Project window with a main [.exe] node and a main [.cpp] node appears.

6. Use the right mouse button to click the main [.exe] node to activate the node's local menu. Select the Add Node menu option to add the file greet.cpp to the project.

The Add to Project List dialog box appears, which enables you to browse for the additional files to be added to the project.

7. After adding the greet [.cpp] node, use the right mouse button to click the main [.exe] node. Select the Make Node menu option to create the simple application.

Project : c:\sample\main.ide

```
greet [.cpp]  code size=31  lines=7  data size=17
main [.cpp]  code size=25  lines=8  data size=0
```

Figure 1.7. *Sample project with two modules.*

8. From the Debug menu, select Run to run the application.

Building More Than One Target

You can follow the general steps outlined in the last section to create projects that build one application from C or C++ modules. Additional files, such as resource scripts (.rc files) or module definition files (.def files) are often included in the project. Sometimes, however, you may need to create more than one target. In projects for the Windows environment, for example, you may need to create a Dynamic Link Library (.DLL file) or a Help File (.HLP file), which is used by the main application. Figure 1.8 illustrates the steps involved and the roles of the Borland C++ tools when creating a DLL and an application using the DLL.

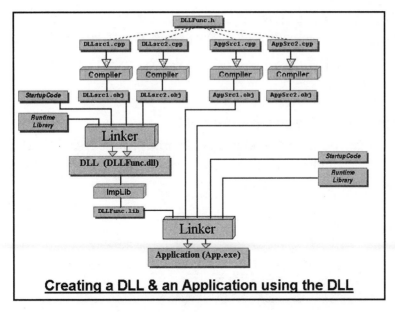

Figure 1.8. *Using a DLL from an application.*

The steps to create a DLL are similar to the ones for creating an application (although the compiler and linker options differ). However, to use the DLL from an application, you must do the following:

- You must create (or obtain) a header file that prototypes the functions or variables provided by the DLL.

- You must include the header file in the application modules that access functions or variables provided by the DLL.

- You must create (or obtain) a copy of an import library for the DLL.

- Include the import library in the link statement of the application using functions or variables from the DLL.

The following section shows you how to create a project with two targets. The steps actually modify the project created earlier (see fig. 1.7).

A Project with Executable and DLL

Suppose that you want to convert the sample project created earlier in this chapter to include a DLL (greet.dll) and an executable (main.exe) that uses the DLL. Follow these steps:

1. Update the files greet.cpp and greet.h to include DLL support as shown in figure 1.9.

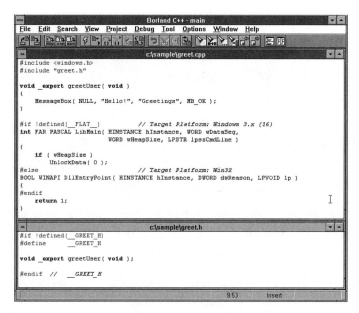

Figure 1.9. *greet.cpp and greet.h updated for DLL support.*

2. From the Project menu, select New Target. The New Target dialog box appears (see fig. 1.10).

Figure 1.10. *The New Target dialog box.*

3. Insert the name of the target (GREET), choose the Standard target type, and select the OK button.

   The Add Target dialog box appears.

4. Select the appropriate target type and library settings for the new DLL. Figure 1.11, for example, illustrates the settings for a Windows 3.x (16) DLL.

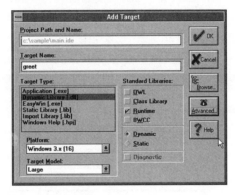

Figure 1.11. *New DLL settings.*

5. Select the **A**dvanced button. The Advanced Options dialog box appears.

6. Turn off the **.rc** and **.d**ef selections and close the dialog boxes using the OK buttons.

7. Use the right mouse button to click on the greet [.cpp] node attached to main [.exe] and choose the Delete Node Local menu option to delete the node.

8. Using the left mouse button, drag the greet [.dll] node and drop it on the main [.exe] node (see fig. 1.12).

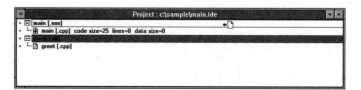

Figure 1.12. *Moving the DLL node to the .exe node.*

9. Use the right mouse button to click on the main [.exe] node to build both the DLL and the executable that uses the DLL. Figure 1.13 shows the project window with the executable and DLL target.

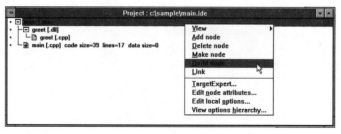

Figure 1.13. *Building an executable and its DLL.*

10. From the Debug menu, select Run to run the application.

You can follow this procedure to create projects with multiple targets, which can be applications, help files, and libraries. A project can have multiple top-level targets, as shown in figure 1.12. Figure 1.13, on the other hand, shows a project with multiple targets but only one top-level target. By moving target nodes, you can instruct the project manager about the dependency rules among your targets.

Lean and Mean Borland C++

Using Command-Line Tools

If you prefer to work at the Windows NT or DOS command prompt, Borland C++ offers command line tools to create libraries and applications. Table 1.1 describes the compilers, linkers, and librarians included with Borland C++.

Table 1.1 Core Command-Line Tools

File Name	Description
BCC.EXE	16-bit compiler. Translates C or C++ modules targeting the DOS or 16-bit Windows environments into object modules.
BCC32.EXE	32-bit compiler. Translates C or C++ modules targeting the Windows NT or Win32s environments into object modules.
TLINK.EXE	16-bit linker. Creates DOS applications and 16-bit Windows applications and dynamic link libraries (DLLs). TLINK.EXE is usually automatically invoked by BCC.EXE. (TLINK.EXE can invoke RLINK.EXE to bind resources to an .EXE or .DLL target)
TLINK32.EXE	32-bit linker. Creates applications or DLLs for the Windows NT or Win32s environments. TLINK32.EXE is usually automatically invoked by BCC32.EXE. (TLINK32.EXE can utilize RLINK32.DLL to bind resources to an .EXE or .DLL target).
TLIB.EXE	Librarian. Creates and maintains static libraries for the DOS, 16-bit Windows, Win32s, and Windows NT environments. TLIB.EXE can also used to add or remove object modules from import libraries.
IMPLIB.EXE	Librarian: Creates an import library from a DLL or a module definition file (.DEF file). Used for both the 16-bit Windows and 32-bit Windows environment.

Configuration Files

The Borland C++ command-line compilers (bcc.exe and bcc32.exe) and linkers (tlink.exe and tlink32.exe) automatically look for configuration files in the current directory and the directory from which they were loaded. Table 1.2 lists the respective configuration file of each tool.

Table 1.2 Compiler and Linker Configuration Files

Tool	Description	Configuration File
BCC.EXE	16-bit Compiler	TURBOC.CFG
BCC32.EXE	32-bit Compiler	BCC32.CFG
TLINK.EXE	16-bit Linker	TLINK.CFG
TLINK32.EXE	32-bit Linker	TLINK32.CFG

The configuration file usually contains your preferred settings for the respective tools. For example, TURBOC.CFG and BCC32.CFG commonly contain the options identifying your include and library directories. Following is an excerpt commonly found in the compiler configuration files:

```
-IE:\BC4\INCLUDE
-LE:\BC4\LIB
-ml
-v
```

Like the compiler configurations, the linker configuration file typically contains the option identifying your library directories:

```
/LE:\BC4\LIB
```

Targeting Windows

The result of your programming efforts targeting the Windows environment is usually an application (EXE) or a dynamic link library (DLL). The following section introduces the steps to create Win16 and Win32 applications and dynamic link libraries using the command-line tools.

Creating a Windows Application

The following code simply displays a greeting message:

```
//////////////////////////////////////////////////////
// SIMPWIN.CPP: A Simple Windows Application...        //
//////////////////////////////////////////////////////
#define STRICT
#include <windows.h>
//
```

```
// Variables for greetings...
//
const char szMsg[] = "Hello from Windows!";
const char szCap[] = "Simple Message";
//
// Application's entry point.
//
#pragma argsused
int PASCAL WinMain( HINSTANCE hInstance,
                    HINSTANCE hPrevInstance,
                    LPSTR lpCmdLine,  int nCmdShow )
{
    // Greet User!
    MessageBox( NULL, szMsg, szCap, MB_OK );
    // Terminate..
    return 0;
}
```

To create the application SIMPWIN.EXE, you must first compile the source SIMPWIN.CPP and then link the resulting object module with the Windows runtime components of Borland C++.

Windows 3.1 (16)

The following command creates a Win16 version of SIMPWIN.EXE:

```
BCC -v -W -ml SIMPWIN.CPP
```

The command invokes the Borland C++ command-line compiler BCC.EXE, which compiles SIMPWIN.CPP and creates SIMPWIN.OBJ. The compiler then automatically invokes the linker, TLINK.EXE, which combines the object module with the runtime modules to create SIMPWIN.EXE.

Win32

The following command creates a Win32 version of SIMPWIN.EXE:

```
BCC32 -v -W  SIMPWIN.CPP
```

The command invokes the Borland C++ command-line compiler
BCC32.EXE, which compiles SIMPWIN.CPP and creates SIMPWIN.OBJ.
The compiler then automatically invokes the linker, TLINK32.EXE,
which combines the object module with the runtime modules to create
SIMPWIN.EXE.

Creating a Windows Dynamic Link Library

To create the dynamic link library, you must first compile the source and then link the resulting object module with the Windows runtime components of Borland C++. The following command performs both steps at once:

```
BCC -v -WD -ml GREET.CPP
```

The command invokes the Borland C++ command-line compiler BCC.EXE, which compiles GREET.CPP and generates GREET.OBJ. The compiler then automatically invokes the linker, TLINK.EXE, which combines the object module with the runtime modules to generate GREET.DLL.

Resource Compilers and Linkers

In general, the user interfaces of Windows programs are defined in resource scripts, which are compiled and linked into the application. You can, for example, use a resource editor to design a dialog box and to assign it a unique identifier. The resource editor produces a dialog box script that is compiled and linked into your application. At runtime, your application can then access and display the dialog box by using the appropriate functions and specifying the dialog's identifier. This allows you to easily modify your user interface without having to modify your code. Other resource types include accelerators, menus, bitmaps, icons, cursors, fonts, version information, and string tables.

Figure 1.14 illustrates steps involved and the roles of the resource compiler and resource linker in the process of using resources in an application.

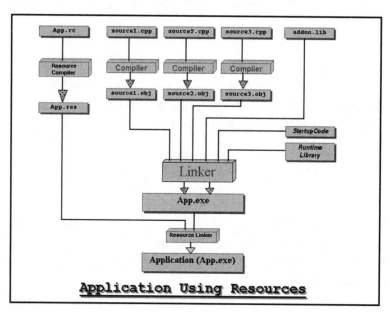

Figure 1.14. *Steps to use resources.*

Table 1.3 describes the Resource Compilers and Linkers included with Borland C++.

Table 1.3 Command-Line Resource Compilers and Linkers

File name	Description
BRCC.EXE	16-bit resource compiler. Translates .RC files into .RES files, which can be linked to applications or DLLs for the 16-bit Windows environments.
RLINK.EXE	16-bit resource linker. Combines one or more .RES files into a 16-bit Windows application (.EXE) or dynamic link library (.DLL).
BRC.EXE	BRC.EXE is a shell that calls BRCC.EXE or RLINK.EXE.
BRCC32.EXE	32-bit resource compiler. Translates .RC files into .RES files, which can be linked to applications or DLLs for the 32-bit Windows environments.
RLINK32.DLL	32-bit resource linker. Combines one or more .RES files into a 32-bit Windows application (.EXE) or dynamic link library (.DLL).

Help Compiler and Tools

Borland C++ includes the Microsoft Help Compiler, HC31.EXE, which allows you to generate a Windows help file (.HLP). Also included is the Multiple Resolution Bitmap Compiler (MRBC.EXE) and the Hot Spot Editor (SHED.EXE). Table 1.4 provides a brief description of these tools.

Table 1.4 Help Compiler and Related Tools

File name	Description
HC31.EXE	Help Compiler. Reads the help project file, the .RTF files, and any specified bitmap (.BMP) or shed (.SHG) files and generates a Windows help (.HLP) file.
MRBC.EXE	Multiple Resolution Bitmap Compiler. Allows you to combine bitmaps of different resolutions into a single file. At runtime, the Windows Help Engine (WINHELP.EXE) automatically loads the appropriate bitmap, based on the screen's resolution.
SHED.EXE	Hotspot Editor. Allows you to create help bitmaps with regions linked to some defined actions. When the user selects one of the regions while viewing the bitmap, the Windows Help Engine performs the associated action, such as displaying a window.

Updating Existing Code for Borland C++

The following section looks at the language and library changes from earlier versions of Borland C++.

Three *char* Types

Borland C++ now recognizes plain *char*, unsigned *char*, and signed *char* as three distinct types. Earlier versions of the compiler treated plain *char* as signed *char*. Consider the following class definitions:

```
class base
{
    public:
        virtual void f( char );
};
class derived : public base
{
    public:
        virtual void f( signed char );
};
```

With earlier versions of the compiler, derived::f(signed char) overrides base::f(char). However, with the new behavior, derived::f(signed char) hides base::f(char).

You can restore the old behavior by using the -K2 switch with the command line compiler. Or, from the IDE you can select the Options menu and then select Project, C++, C++ Compatibility and enable the Don't Treat Char As A Distinct Type option.

Array Version of the New and Delete Operators

Borland C++ now uses operator new[] and operator delete[] for allocating and deallocating storage for arrays of objects. If you provide custom versions of the non-array version of operator new and operator delete, you should probably provide new definitions for the array versions, too.

Operator New and Exceptions

The default new_handler provided with Borland C++ behaves according to the ANSI C++ specification and throws an xalloc exception to indicate an allocation failure. Therefore, any code checking for a zero return value from operator new has to be updated. The following example illustrates the necessary change:

```
/////////////////////////////////////////////////////
// NEWNEW.CPP: xalloc exception and the new operator //
/////////////////////////////////////////////////////
#include <new.h>
const int size = 0x100;
//
// Old method to check for memory allocation failures...
//
void old_func( void )
{
    char *p;
    if ( !( p = new char[size] ) )
    {
        // Memory Allocation Failure...
    }
    else
    {
        // Successful Memory Allocation
        // ...
    }
    // ...
}
//
// New method to check for memory allocation failures
//
```

```
void new_func( void )
{
    char *p;
    try
    {
        p = new char[size];
        // Successful Memory Allocation
        // ...
    }
    catch( xalloc& xx )
    {
        // Memory Allocation Failure...
    }
    // ...
}
```

Using the *longjmp* and *setjmp* Functions

The definition of the jmp_buf type used by the setjmp and longjmp functions has changed to accommodate the support for exception handling. The following listing illustrates the old and new definitions:

```
//                              //
// Prior definition            // New definition
// of jmp_buf                  // of jmp_buff
//                              //
typedef struct __jmp_buf {      typedef struct __jmp_buf {
    unsigned    j_sp;               unsigned    j_sp;
    unsigned    j_ss;               unsigned    j_ss;
    unsigned    j_flag;             unsigned    j_flag;
    unsigned    j_cs;               unsigned    j_cs;
```

```
      unsigned    j_ip;                    unsigned    j_ip;
      unsigned    j_bp;                    unsigned    j_bp;
      unsigned    j_di;                    unsigned    j_di;
      unsigned    j_es;                    unsigned    j_es;
      unsigned    j_si;                    unsigned    j_si;
      unsigned    j_ds;                    unsigned    j_ds;
}     jmp_buf[1];                          unsigned    j_excep;
                                           unsigned    j_context;
                                     }     jmp_buf[1];
```

Renamed Global Variables

Table 1.5 lists various global variables from the Borland C++ runtime library that have been renamed.

Table 1.5 Rename Global Variables

Old Names	New Names
daylight	_daylight
directvideo	_directvideo
environ	_environ
timezone	_timezone
tzname	_tzname
sys_errlist	_sys_errlist
sys_nerr	_sys_nerr

Tip: Using obsolete.lib

If your programs use the variables listed in Table 1.5, you should update the references to reflect the new names. If, however, you have an object module or library that refers to the old names and cannot be modified, add the library obsolete.lib to your project (or the library list when calling the command-line linkers) to resolve any undefined symbol error messages.

Summary

In this chapter, you have learned how to use the Borland C++ tools to generate applications from C or C++ source code. The following chapters of this book focus on the syntax, constructs, and idioms commonly used in C or C++ code. You will have ample material to practice the steps to compile code snippets or projects.

Chapter 2
The C Language

Borland C++ fully supports the standard for the C language as documented by the American National Standards Institute (ANSI). This chapter introduces you to the elements and syntax of ANSI C via example programs or small snippets of code. Given that C++ evolved from C, a good understanding of the C language is a prerequisite for adequate C++ programming. This chapter looks at a simple program, which traditionally has been the first program of novice C programmers.

A Simple C Program

The following short example illustrates the basic structure of a C program.

```c
/* HELLO.C: A sample C example */
#include <stdio.h>
int main( void )
{
    printf( "Hello World" );
    return 0;
}
```

If you are using the IDE, you need to create a project for this sample program. The steps for creating a project are as follows:

1. From the **P**roject menu, select New Project.

   The New Project dialog box appears.

2. Enter a project name in the **P**roject Path and Name field. You might, for example, type **hello** or **c:\bc4\examples\hello**.

   The **T**arget Name field will automatically contain "HELLO," the last word in the **P**roject Path and Name field.

3. From the Target Type list, choose EasyWin (.exe).

   The Project Manager automatically sets the P**l**atform to Windows 3.x (16). The Target **M**odel is set to Small, and the Standard Libraries is set to **S**tatic, as shown in figure 2.1.

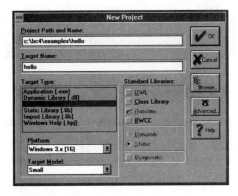

Figure 2.1. *The New Project dialog box.*

4. Select the **Advanced** button on the right side of the dialog box to further customize the project. The New Target Options dialog box appears.

5. Select only the **.c** node from the list of Initial Nodes, as shown in figure 2.2.

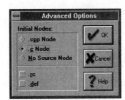

Figure 2.2. *The Advanced Options dialog box.*

6. Choose OK and OK again to close both dialog boxes.

You have now started a new project with a project window containing several nodes, including a hello.c node. Figure 2.3 shows a sample project window.

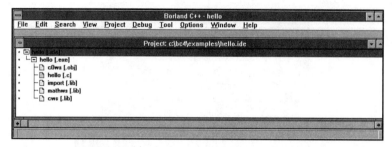

Figure 2.3. *The project window.*

Tip: Customizing the Project Window

You may not see all the nodes shown in figure 2.3 if you have not enabled the runtime nodes and project node. Similarly, each one of your project nodes may display more or less information depending on your Project View settings. To customize the project window, from the Options menu, select Environment. Then select Project View.

Double-click on the hello.c node in the Project window and enter the above code for the sample program in the editor window. Save the code to disk by choosing **S**ave from the **F**ile menu.

You are now ready to compile, link, and run the program. From the **Pr**oject menu, choose Make All. The Compile Status dialog box appears. If you encounter any errors, verify that the code was correctly typed.

After compiling and linking the code successfully, you need to run it. From the **D**ebug menu, select Run. When the program is run, it displays the words Hello, world in a window.

If you prefer the command-line tools to the IDE, use your preferred text editor to save the sample as HELLO.C. To complile the program, if you are a DOS user, use the command **bcc hello.c.** If you are a Windows NT user, use the command **bcc32 hello.c** to compile the program.

Compiling creates the program HELLO.EXE, which you can run by typing **hello** and pressing Enter. The program displays the words `Hello, world.`

Components of the Program

Let's take a closer look at the components of this little program.

Comments

The example program begins with a comment. A *comment* is a section of code that is ignored by the compiler. The forward slash and asterisk combination (/*) starts a comment. The compiler ignores every character until it encounters the asterisk and backslash combination (*\).

Tip: C++-Style Comments in C Mode

Borland C++ also supports the C++ style of comments when you write C code. In C++, a comment begins with two forward slashes (//) and goes to the end of the line. You should avoid using C++-style comments if you intend to port your C code to another environment because other C compilers may not support // comments.

#include and Header Files

The #include instruction that follows the comment tells the compiler to insert the contents of the file stdio.h in the sample. stdio.h is one of the many include or header files supplied with the Borland C++ compiler. *Header files* provide the compiler with information about functions and data that you can use in your program.

The main Function

The next section of the sample program is the function main. Strictly speaking, every C program contains this function, which is also the starting point of the program. Programs targeting the Windows environment, however, often have a WinMain function instead of the main function.

Format of a Function

The general format of a function is as follows:

```
<return type> FunctionName( parameters )
{
    // Here goes the function body
    // made up of statements
}
```

If you look at a whole C program as an essay, a function can be viewed as a paragraph in the essay. Each function is, in turn, made up of statements, which are like sentences. Each statement ends with a semicolon (;).

The simple program hello is made up of only one function, which contains two statements. The first statement prints a greeting message using the printf function. The second statement returns the value zero (0) to the caller of the function.

Functions often return the result of a computation. It is customary for the function main to return the value of zero to indicate that no errors were encountered.

Representing Information in C

Strictly speaking, a program processes information or data. The hello program processed the greeting message by displaying it. C provides several ways to represent information or data.

Constants

Generically, a *constant* refers to any value that cannot be modified. C supports string constants, character constants, integer constants, and floating-point constants.

A *string constant* is a series of characters enclosed in double quotation marks. The hello program uses the constant string "Hello, world".

C also supports *character constants*, *integer constants*, and *floating-point* constants. The table 2.1 describes their respective format.

Table 2.1 C Constants

Constant	Format	Example
Character	Enclosed by single quotation mark	'a', '!'
Integer	Decimal: A series of digits not beginning with 0	123, 989
	Octal: 0 followed by octal digits	077, 023
	Hex: 0x or 0X followed by hexadecimal digits.	0xAF, 0x9B
Float	Decimal: [digits].[digits]	1., .34, 2.5
	Exponential: [digit][E|e][+|-]digits	4e7, 5e+8
String	"character, character, ..."	"Hello", "C \n"

Simple Data Types

C provides several data types that you can create to store information while processing data. Each type occupies a number of bytes in memory and may represent values in a predefined range. The size and range of a given type may not be the same for different programming environments. Table 2.2 outlines the basic types available to programs targeting the DOS or Windows 16-bit environments.

Table 2.2 Simple Data Types

Data Type	Size	Range
char	8	-128 to 127
signed char	8	-128 to 127
unsigned char	8	0 to 255
short int	16	-32,768 to 32,767
unsigned int	16	0 to 65,535
int	16	-32,768 to 32,767
long	32	-2,147,483,648 to 2,147,483,647
unsigned long	32	0 to 4,294,967,295
float	32	3.4×10^{-38} to 3.4×10^{38}
double	64	1.7×10^{-308} to 1.7×10^{308}
long double	80	3.4×10^{-4932} to 1.1×10^{4932}

Tip: Using limits.h and float.h To Find Data Type Range

You can use the macros defined in the header files limits.h and floats.h to determine the data range of various data types at compile time. This permits your code to remain portable across different environments.

Variables

To set aside memory of a particular type, you declare a *variable*. First, state the data type and then a variable name, as shown:

```
int  i;                 //declare integer i
long l=10;              //declare and initialize long l
double d1, d2, d3=1.25; //set aside mem. for 3 doubles
```

You can provide an initial value when declaring a variable. You also can declare more that one variable of a single type by separating each variable name with a comma. As with other C statements, the declaration is terminated with a semicolon (;).

Typed Constants

Typed constants are variables that cannot be modified. You can create a typed constant by using the syntax for declaring and initializing a variable and preceding the type with the *const* keyword. The following sample makes use of a typed constant:

```
/* ************************************************ */
/* CONST.C: This example uses both a Macro and a    */
/*          typed constant...                       */
/* ************************************************ */
#include <stdio.h>
#define GERMAN_PRICE   10        /* Use macro for constant */
const float xchgRate = 1.60;     /* Use typed constant!    */
int main( void )
{
    printf( "This product costs $%.2f in the USA!",
                GERMAN_PRICE * xchgRate );

    return 0;
}
```

Functions

You are now somewhat familiar with two functions: main and printf. You have written the first one and called the second to display messages. While learning a programming language, it is useful to be conversant with the input and output (I/O) routines. The I/O routines enable you to monitor the behavior, direction, and status of your programs by displaying messages and the contents of variables.

Input and Output

You have seen the printf function used to display messages. printf is always called with at least one string as an argument. The function scans the string and displays every character verbatim until it encounters a conversion specification.

Conversion Specification

A *conversion specification* starts with a percent sign (%) and has the following format:

```
%[flag][width][.prec][size_modifier]type
```

Each conversion specification prompts printf to look for an additional argument, which is formatted and displayed as dictated by the conversion specification. You must ensure that you call printf with an additional argument for each conversion specification specified.

Table 2.3 sums up the components of a conversion specification.

Table 2.3 Conversion Specification for printf

Component	Optional	Char.	Specifies
flags	Yes	–	Left justify within the field
		0	Use 0 for padding instead of spaces
		+	Forces + or – to always be displayed
		blank	Use leading space if value is positive
		#	Prepend 0 to octal value Prepend 0x to hexadecimal value
width	Yes		Minimum field width
prec	Yes		Maximum number of characters to be printed; for integers, minimum number of digits to print

continues

Table 2.3 continued

Component	Optional	Char.	Specifies
size_mod	Yes	F	Input is a far pointer
		N	Input is a near pointer
		h	Input is short int
		l	Input is long int
		L	Input is long double
type_char	No	d	Format as a signed decimal integer
		i	Same as 'd'
		o	Format as octal unsigned int
		u	Format as unsigned decimal
		x	Format as unsigned hex. with lowercase
		X	Format as unsigned hex. with uppercase
		f	Signed float with [-]dddd.dddd
		e	Signed float with [-]d.dddd or e[+/-]ddd
		g	Signed value (use 'f' or 'e' form
		E	Signed float with [-]d.dddd or E[+/-]ddd
		G	Signed float (use 'f' or 'E' form)
		c	Displays single character

Component	Optional	Char.	Specifies
		s	Displays null-terminated string
		n	Displays pointer to int
		p	Pointer with SSSS:OOOO or OOOO

The following example will give you a good feel for the power and flexibility of printf:

```c
/* ************************************************* */
/* PRINTF.C: Example displaying versatility &        */
/*          flexibility of the printf function...    */
/* ************************************************* */
#include <stdio.h>
int main( void )
{
    int    i=11;
    float  f=500.78653;
    printf( "Hello, world!\n" );    /* Print String */
    /* Print several strings... */
    printf( "%s, %s!\n", "Hello", "again" );
    /* Display integer in various formats... */
    printf( "Integer = (dec)%d, (oct)%#o, (hex)%#x \n", i, i, i );
    /* Width and precision control... */
    printf( "Float   = %f, %6.2f \n", f, f );
    /* Left justification and '0' padding' */
    printf( "%-7.2f+ %d = %08.2f\n", f, i, f+i );
        return 0;
}
```

Escape Sequences

The backslash character (\) has a special meaning in C. It is referred to as the *escape character*. It is used to represent characters or numbers that cannot be easily entered with the keyboard. For example, the Backspace or Enter key perform special functions while you're editing. To represent them in your program, you can use an *escape sequence*: an escape code following the escape character. Table 2.4 lists the escape sequences you can use in your C program.

Table 2.4 Escape Sequences

Sequence	Name	Function
\a	Bell/Alert	Beeps
\b	Backspace	Backs up one character
\f	Form feed	Starts new screen
\n	New line	Moves to beginning of next line
\r	Carriage return	Moves to beginning of current line
\t	Horizontal tab	Moves to next tab position
\v	Vertical tab	Moves cursor down
\\	Backslash	Displays backslash character
\'	Single quotation mark	Displays a single quotation mark
\"	Double quotation mark	Displays a double quotation mark

An escape character can also be used to represent a character's value in hexadecimal or octal format. Table 2.5 lists character values using escape sequences.

Table 2.5 Character Value Using Escape Sequences

Format	Base	Description
\OOO	Octal	One to three octal digits following the escape character
\xHHH or \XHHH	Hexadecimal	One or two hexadecimal digits following the escape character and x or X

printf will correctly format escape sequences embedded within the format string, providing for more flexible formatting. You have seen '\n' used in several of the calls to printf.

The Functions scanf, gets, atoi, atol, and atof

The counterpart to printf is the scanf function. Just like printf, scanf expects a string that contains one or more *format specifiers* indicating the format and type of data to be read in. The additional parameters following the format string must be the address of the variables in which the data is to be stored.

Unlike printf, however, scanf is often sidestepped by programmers. If the input read by scanf does not match the format string, the function may behave unexpectedly. Because you cannot always assume that the users of your program will enter data in the expected format, you may opt to use the gets function instead of the powerful, but unforgiving, scanf. *gets* reads a line of data into a specified buffer. The data is read in as a string. If you are expecting a number, you then can use the atoi, atol, or atof functions to convert the string to an integer, a long, or a float respectively. Following is an example:

```c
/* ************************************************** */
/* IN_OUT.C: Sample illustrating Input/Output...      */
/* ************************************************** */
#include <stdio.h>  /* stdio.h declares printf/gets */
#include <stdlib.h> /* stdlib.h prototypes atoi      */
int main( void )
{
    char name[80],  /* char array to receive name   */
        ageStr[80]; /* char array to receive age..  */
    int  age = 0 ;  /* int to receive age..         */
    /* Prompt user to enter name */
    printf( "Please enter your name: " );
    /* Read input in name array  */
    gets( name );
    /* Greet user! Ask for user's age */
    printf( "Hello %s! Are old are you? ", name );
    /* Read user's age as a string..*/
    gets( ageStr );
    /* Convert string to integer... */
    age = atoi( ageStr );
    /* If user entered valid number.*/
    if ( age != 0 )
            /* Display user's age */
            printf( "Wow, %d yrs old!", age );
    else
            /* Inform user we understand.. */
            printf( "Ok, We won't talk about it" );
    return 0;
}
```

Sample Function

Now that you have methods to receive and display data, the following sections work toward putting together some simple functions.

Function Prototype

It is common for a function to be declared before it is defined. The declaration step informs the compiler of the existence of the function—its return type as well as the parameters it expects. A *function declaration* is also often called a *function prototype*. The general format of a function declaration is as follows:

```
<return type> FunctionName( parameters );
```

Following are some general characteristics of function prototypes:

- The return type may be one of the data types you have seen earlier (or a user-defined type). Functions that do not return data usually have a return type of void.

- The parameters usually specify each variable type and variable name, separated by commas. The variable name is not necessary when prototyping a function, although it is usually included.

- Like the return type, functions that do not expect any parameters or arguments are prototyped with the keyword "void" in the parameter list.

Suppose that you have been assigned the task of writing a function that returns the average of three values. The first decision you need to make is the proper data type to represent the numbers. Glancing at the data type table, you decide to be safe and use long integers because the values may exceed the range of regular integers. So you use the following function prototype:

```
long  Average( long val1, long val2, long val3 );
```

This informs the compiler that the function *Average* expects three long values and also returns a long result. Next, you define the function body.

Function Definition

The following is a plausible implementation of the Average function:

```
/* Average, Function definition  */
long Average( long val1, long val2, long val3 )
{
    long sum = val1 + val2 + val3;
    return sum/3;
}
```

To confirm that this code is correct, you decide to prompt the user for three values and to display the average. Fair enough. In the name of caution, you decide to avoid the scanf function and opt for the safer gets/atol combination. Because you will prompt the user for a long value more than once, you decide to localize the prompting routine in a function, appropriately called readLong. Following is the result:

```
/* *********************************************** */
/* AVGNUM.C: Function computing average of 3 numbers */
/* *********************************************** */
#include <stdio.h>
#include <stdlib.h>
/* Function Prototypes */
long Average( long val1, long val2, long val3 );
long ReadLong( void );
/* Average, Function definition  */
long Average( long val1, long val2, long val3 )
{
    long sum = val1 + val2 + val3;
    return sum/3;
}
/* ReadLong, Function definition  */
long ReadLong( void )
{
    char buffer[80];
    gets( buffer );          /* read string.. */
    return atol( buffer );   /* string->long  */
}
int main( void )
{
    long l1, l2, l3, avg;
    printf( "Please enter first  value: " );
    l1 = ReadLong();
    printf( "Please enter second value: " );
    l2 = ReadLong();
    printf( "Please enter third  value: " );
    l3 = ReadLong();
    avg = Average( l1, l2, l3 );
```

```
    printf( "The average of the values= %ld \n", avg );
    return 0;
}
```

Expressions and Operators

A function commonly contains one or more expressions that manipulate
data or compute a value. The Average function uses the + operator to
add values. C provides a rich group of operators that you can use to
express the operations performed by your function. When an expression
contains more than one operator, the order of precedence determines
the sequence in which the operators take effect. As expected, expressions with higher precedence operators are evaluated first. Operators
with similar precedence are evaluated according to their associativity.
Table 2.6 lists operators along with a short description, precedence, and
associativity.

Table 2.6 C Operators

Operator	Description	Example	Precedence/ Associativity
		Primary and Postfix	
[]	array subscript	columns[5]	16, left to right
()	function call	printf(msg)	16, left to right
.	member ref	time.tm_hour	16, left to right
->	member ptr	time->tm_hour	16, left to right
++	postfix increment	counter++	15, left to right
--	postfix decrement	counter--	15, left to right

Operator	Description	Example	Precedence/Associativity
		Unary Operators	
++	prefix increment	++counter	14, right to left
––	prefix decrement	––counter	14, right to left
sizeof	size in bytes	sizeof(custRec)	14, right to left
(type)	cast	(float)i	14, right to left
~	bitwise not	~WS_VISIBLE	14, right to left
!	logical not	!EOF	14, right to left
-	unary minus	-i	14, right to left
&	address of	&aVar	14, right to left
*	indirection	*ptr	14, right to left
		Binary & Ternary Operators	
		Multiplicative	
*	multiplication	aVar*10	13, left to right
/	division	aVar/10	13, left to right
%	modulus	aVar%10	13, left to right
		Additive	
+	addition	aVar+20	12, left to right
-	subtraction	aVar-20	12, left to right
		Bitwise Shift	
<<	left shift	aVar << 1	11, left to right
>>	right shift	aVar >> 1	11, left to right

continues

Table 2.6 continued

Operator	Description	Example	Precedence/ Associativity
		Relational	
<	less than	i < counter	10, left to right
>	greater than	i > limit	10, left to right
		Equality	
==	equal	value == 0	9, left to right
!=	not equal to	value != 0	9, left to right
		Bitwise	
&	bitwise AND	style & WS_BORDER	8, left to right
^	bitwise XOR	flag ^ msk	7, left to right
|	bitwise OR	style | WS_VISIBLE	6, left to right
		Logical	
&&	logical AND	!EOF && sizeRead>0	5, left to right
||	logical OR	a==0 || b==0	4, left to right
		Conditional	
? :	conditional	a>b ? 1 : 0	3, right to left
		Assignment	
=	assignment	x = 10	2, right to left
*=	assign multiply	x *=10	2, right to left
/=	assign divide	x /=10	2, right to left

Operator	Description	Example	Precedence/Associativity
%=	assign modulo	x %=10	2, right to left
+=	assign add	x +=10	2, right to left
-=	assign subtract	x -=10	2, right to left
<<=	assign shift left	var <<= 100	2, right to left
>>=	assign shift right	var >>= 100	2, right to left
&=	assign AND	i &= j	2, right to left
^=	assign XOR	i ^= j	2, right to left
|=	assign OR	i |= j	2, right to left
,	comma	x=2, y=3	1, left to right

The following sample code uses a few operators:

```
/* ************************************************* */
/* OPERATOR.C: Sample using some C operators...      */
/* ************************************************* */
#include <stdio.h>
#include <stdlib.h>
int main( void )
{
  int i1=10, i2=20;
  /* sizeof operator... */
  printf( "Size of an int is %d bytes \n", sizeof( int ) );
  printf( "Size of a long is %d bytes \n", sizeof( float ));
  /* shift operators... */
  printf( "%d * 2= %d   and   %d << 1 = %d\n", i1, i1*2,
                                         i1, i1<<1 );
  printf( "%d / 2= %d   and   %d << 1 = %d\n", i2, i2/2,
                                         i2, i2>>1 );

  return 0;
}
```

Conditional Statements and Loops

Until now, all the example programs have executed in a linear fashion. Every statement is carried out exactly once in the order it is encountered. You have probably noticed that this approach is rather limiting. The types of problems you need to solve require that your program "make decisions." C provides various constructs to allow you to control the flow of your program's execution. You can, for example, determine whether a statement should be executed by checking for the validity of a condition. For even more control, you can also combine various statements into a block and treat the block as a single statement.

A *block* starts with an opening brace ({) and ends with a closing brace (}). A function in itself is a block and it is not uncommon to encounter the term *function block*.

Using if and else Statements

The if statement allows conditional branching by evaluating whether an expression or combination of expressions is true. The syntax is as follows:

```
if ( expression )
    statement_to_be_executed_if_expression_is_true;
```

The following code illustrates the use of the if statement with a simple statement:

```
/* ********************************************** */
/* IF.C: Conditional branching using if( ... )    */
/* ********************************************** */
#include    <stdio.h>        // Prototypes printf()
#include    <dos.h>          // Prototypes _dos_gettime()
int main( void )
{
```

```
    struct  time t;
     _dos_gettime( &t );
     if ( t.ti_hour < 12 )
         printf( "Good Morning! " );
     if ( t.ti_hour >= 12 )
         printf( "Good Afternoon! " );
    printf( "It is now: %2d:%02d:%02d\n",
             t.ti_hour, t.ti_min, t.ti_sec );
    return 0;
}
```

You may optionally use the else keyword in combination with the if
statement. else allows an alternate statement to be executed if the
expression is not true. Following is the same example code, simplified
with the if/else combination:

```
/* *********************************************** */
/* IFELSE.C: Conditional branching with if/else...   */
/* *********************************************** */
#include    <stdio.h>        // Prototypes printf()
#include    <dos.h>          // Prototypes _dos_gettime()
int main( void )
{
    struct  time t;
     _dos_gettime( &t );
     if ( t.ti_hour < 12 )
         printf( "Good Morning! " );
     else
         printf( "Good Afternoon! " );
    printf( "It is now: %2d:%02d:%02d\n",
             t.ti_hour, t.ti_min, t.ti_sec );
    return 0;
}
```

You can nest the if and else statements. The compiler pairs each else with the closest if when the usage is ambiguous. Consider the following example:

```
/* ************************************************* */
/* IFELSE1.C: Illustrates nesting if/else statements */
/* ************************************************* */
#define NOWORK_RATE 0
#define NORMAL_RATE 1
#define DOUBLE_RATE 2
const float hrlyRate = 6.00;
float GetDayEarnings( int hours )
{
    int rate = NORMAL_RATE;    /* Assume default Rate   */
    if ( hours > 0 )           /* Check Attendance...   */
        if ( hours > 8 )       /* Worked O.T. ?         */
            rate = DOUBLE_RATE;
    else
        rate = NOWORK_RATE;
    return  hrlyRate * hours * rate;
}
```

This example needs braces because the else is paired with the inner if, which results in incorrect logic. The corrected version follows:

```
/* ************************************************* */
/* IFELSE2.C: Illustrates nesting if/else statements */
/* ************************************************* */
#define NOWORK_RATE 0
#define NORMAL_RATE 1
#define DOUBLE_RATE 2
const float hrlyRate = 6.00;
float GetDayEarnings( int hours )
{
    int rate = NORMAL_RATE;    /* Assume default Rate   */
    if ( hours > 0 )           /* Check Attendance...   */
    {
```

```
        if ( hours > 8 )            /* Worked O.T. ?        */
            rate = DOUBLE_RATE;
    }
    else
        rate = NOWORK_RATE;
    return  hrlyRate * hours * rate;
}
```

Using switch and case Statements

Your program may sometimes reach a point where more than two
alternate routes are possible. You may, for example, design a menu that
offers the user a choice of several commands. To properly branch in
these complex conditions, you can use a series of if/else statements, as
follows:

```
void ProcessBBSMenu()
{
    char option = GetSelectedOption();
    option = toupper( option );
    if      ( option == 'F' )
        FileMenu();
    else if ( option == 'M' )
        MessageMenu();
    else if ( option == 'G' )
        LogOffUser();
    else
        ShowOptions();
}
```

Alternatively, C offers the switch and case keywords for complex conditional execution. The syntax for these keywords is as follows:

```
switch ( expression )
{
```

```
case constant_expression:   statement or group of statements
case constant_expression:   statement or group of statements
...
default: statement or group of statements
}
```

The result of the *expression* is compared against the *constant_expression* of each case. If a match is found, control is transferred to the statement(s) associated with the case. Note that execution proceeds until the end of the switch body or until a break statement transfers control out of the body.

The statements associated with the default keyword are executed if the expression does not match any of the cases. The default is optional and does not have to be at the end.

The example ProcessBBSMenu function can be rewritten to take advantage of the switch statement, as follows:

```
void ProcessBBSMenu()
{
    switch( GetSelectedOption() )
    {
        default: ShowOptions();
        case 'f':
        case 'F': FileMenu();
                break;
        case 'm':
        case 'M': MessageMenu();
                break;
        case 'g':
        case 'G': LogOffUser();
                break;
    }
}
```

Using the while Keyword

The while keyword allows a statement or block to be repeated until a specified condition is no longer true. The syntax is as follows:

```
while ( expression )
    statement
```

The statement or body associated with the while loop will not be executed if the expression is initially false. The following example illustrates the use of the while statement in a routine that simply waits for a specified amount of time:

```
/* ************************************************ */
/* WHILE.C:  Example illustrating the use of a while */
/*           loop...                               */
/* ************************************************ */
#include <stdio.h>
#include <time.h>
void WaitFor( int secs )
{
    time_t start = time( NULL ), now = start;
    while( now < start+secs )
        now = time( NULL );
}
int main( void )
{
    printf( "Waiting for 5 seconds..." );
    WaitFor( 5 );
    printf( "\nDone!" );
    return 0;
}
```

Using the Null Statement

You probably have noticed that the while loop in the CopyString function does not have any statement or body attached. Actually it does! A lonely semicolon (;) is a statement and is referred to as the *null statement*. Use the null statement whenever a statement is expected but you don't need any code to be executed.

Using the for Keyword

The for loop is similar to the while loop with two enhancements:

- You can specify an initialization statement that is executed once before the conditional expression is evaluated.

- You can provide an expression that is executed after each iteration of the statement or body attached to the for loop.

The syntax is as follows:

```
for (initialization; conditional_expr.; post_expr.)
    statement or group of statements
```

You should note that all three possible expressions are optional. The initialization expression, if provided, will always be executed; the post_expression may not be evaluated if the conditional expression is initially false. The following sample is a modified version of the WaitFor function using the for loop:

```
/* ************************************************** */
/* FOR.C:  Example illustrating a for loop...         */
/* ************************************************** */
#include <stdio.h>
#include <time.h>
void WaitFor( int secs )
{
    time_t start;
    for( start=time( NULL ); time( NULL ) < start+secs;    )
    ;    // Null Statement...
}
int main( void )
{
    printf( "Waiting for 5 seconds..." );
    WaitFor( 5 );
    printf( "\nDone!" );
    return 0;
}
```

This example does not provide a post-iteration expression and has a null statement for its body.

Using a do/while Loop

In a do/while loop, the conditional expression is evaluated after the body of the loop is executed. This means that the statement or body of statements associated with the loop is always executed at least once. The syntax is as follows:

```
do statement or group of statements
while (expression)
```

You will find the do/while loop useful when you need to prompt the user whether a particular operation should be repeated. Following is an example:

```
/* ************************************************* */
/* DOWHILE.C: Sample using a do/while loop to carry  */
/*            a task and prompt user for response..  */
/* ************************************************* */
#include <stdio.h>
#include <conio.h>
#include <dos.h>
/* Prototype(s)        */
void ShowInfo( void );
/* ShowInfo: Displays some system information   */
void ShowInfo( void )
{
    clrscr();
    printf( "OS Version: %d.%02d \n", _osmajor, _osminor );
    printf( "PSP       : %X\n", _psp );
}
int main( void )
{
    int answer;
    do{
        ShowInfo();
        printf( "Do you want to exit ?" );
        answer = getch();
    } while( answer != 'Y' && answer != 'y' );
    printf( "Done...\n" );
    return 0;
}
```

Interrupting a Block

It is sometimes necessary to unconditionally jump out of a block of
statements. C provides various keywords for that purpose: break, continue, and return.

The break statement stops the execution of the nearest enclosing while, do/while, for, or switch statement. You can provide better error checking within a loop by issuing a break when an unexpected condition is detected. Suppose that you need to save a very long list of first names and last names. You can take advantage of the never-ending while loop to prompt the user for information and then use the break statement to terminate the loop when the user has no more data to enter. Following is a possible implementation:

```c
/* *********************************************** */
/* BREAK.C: Uses 'break' to terminate loop...      */
/* *********************************************** */
#include <stdio.h>
/* Save names away */
void SaveInput( char *firstName, char *lastName )
{
    /* To be implemented!   */
}
/* Retrieves first/last name until no info is entered.*/
void ProcessInput( void )
{
  char fname[80];
  char lname[80];
  while( 1 )
  {
      printf( "Enter first name: " );
      if ( !gets( fname ) ¦¦ !fname[0] )  /* Verify Input!*/
          break;                          /* Exit loop!   */
      printf( "Enter last name : " );
      if ( !gets( lname ) ¦¦ !lname[0] )  /* Verify Input!*/
          break;                          /* Exit loop!   */
      SaveInput( fname, lname );
  }
}
int main( void )
{
```

```
  ProcessInput();
  printf( "Done..." );
  return 0;
}
```

The continue statement is very similar to break with two differences:

- continue does not affect switch statements.

- continue goes back to the beginning of the loop after bypassing the
  rest of the loop.

The following example calls the random function in a loop until 10 odd
numbers are found. Each time an even number is generated, the continue statement is used to transfer control back to the beginning of the
loop:

```
/* ************************************************* */
/* CONTINUE.C: Sample illustrating 'continue'.       */
/* ************************************************* */
#include <stdlib.h>
#include <stdio.h>
#include <time.h>
/* Function prototype. */
void InitRoutine( void );
void InitRoutine()
{
```

```
        printf( "Performing initialization...\n" );
        randomize();
}
int main( void )
{
    int count=0;
    for( InitRoutine(); count<10;   )
    {
        int val = random( 100 );
        if ( val % 2 == 0 )
        {
            putchar( '.' );
            continue;
        }
        count++;
        printf( "\nOdd number found: %d ", val );
    }
    return 0;
}
```

You can use a return statement with an optional return expression or return value to terminate a function. The syntax is as follows:

```
return expression;
```

Functions declared as void don't return values. If missing, a return statement is implied after the last statement in a function. However, the return value is undefined in this case.

Using goto and label Statements

A goto statement allows unconditional transfer of control to a label within the current function. The syntax is as follows:

```
goto label
```

label is the identifier name used in a statement with the identifier followed by a colon (:).

> **Tip:** goto: A Necessary Evil
>
> Although the goto keyword is permitted in C, you should be aware that its usage is discouraged in favor of conditional or iteration statements. Actually, you should even the break and continue statements if possible. Unconditional branching often results in code that is hard to understand. However, goto is commonly used when an unexpected or error condition is encountered inside a deeply nested loop. Using goto in these circumstances often keeps the code simpler.

Variable Scope

The scope of a variable refers to the area in the program where the variable is accessible or usable.

Local Variables

The functions you have seen declared variables within a function definition or function block. These variables are referred to as local variables and can be accessed only from within the function or block they are declared. In the following example, var1 is accessible from only func( ); var2 is active only within main( ):

```
/* ************************************************ */
/* SCOPE1.C: Illustrates scope of local variables... */
/* ************************************************ */
```

```
#include <stdio.h>
void func( void )
{
    int var1 = 11;       /* Local variable, var1 */
    printf( "In func() with var1=%d\n", var1 );
}
int main( void )
{
    int var2= 22;        /* Local variable, var2 */
    printf( "In main() with var2=%d\n", var2 );
    func();
    /* Line commented out since main() cannot access var1
       resulting in an 'Undefined symbol var1' error...

    printf( "In main() with var1=%d\n", var1 );
    */
    return 0;
}
```

Global Variables

A variable declared outside of any function is referred to as a *global variable* and is accessible from its point of declaration to the end of the file. To make var1 accessible to both func() and main(), for example, you can declare the variable at the top of the file, as illustrated in the following example:

```
/* ************************************************ */
/* SCOPE2.C: Illustrates scope of local/global var.  */
/* ************************************************ */
#include <stdio.h>
int var1 = 11;       /* Global variable, var1 */
void func( void )
```

```
{
    printf( "In func() with var1=%d\n", var1 );
}
int main( void )
{
    int var2= 22;    /* Local variable, var2 */
    printf( "In main() with var2=%d\n", var2 );
    func();
    printf( "In main() with var1=%d\n", var1 );
    return 0;
}
```

Variable Visibility

Local variable definition is not restricted to the beginning of a function. You can declare a local variable at the beginning of a block. The scope of the variable extends to the end of the block. A variable declared in a block "hides" any other variable with a similar name declared outside the block. In the following program, for example, the printf( ) calls display three different values for the variable var1:

```
/* ************************************************ */
/* SCOPE3.C: Illustrates scope of local/global var.  */
/* ************************************************ */
#include <stdio.h>
int var1 = 12;        /* Global variable, var1 */
int main( void )
{
  if ( printf( "Entering outer if() block \n" ) )
  {
    int var1 = 34;
    printf( "In outer if() block, var1=%d\n", var1 );
    if ( printf( "Entering inner if() block \n" ) )
```

```
  {
    int var1 = 56;
    printf( "In inner if() block, var1=%d\n", var1 );
  }
}
printf( "In main(), var1=%d\n", var1 );
return 0;
}
```

The first two calls have local copies of var1 defined within their respective blocks. The last one displays the global copy of var1.

Variable Duration

The memory for local variables is set aside when the function starts. Once the function returns, the memory is available and can be used by other functions. Therefore, you should not expect the data stored in a local variable to remain unchanged when calling the function multiple times. If, however, you need the value of a local variable to be preserved between calls to the function, you can use the static modifier when declaring the variable. The static keyword gives the local variable permanent storage.

Variable Modifiers

The C language provides several modifiers, such as static, which alter the scope and duration or storage of variables. Table 2.7 describes the various modifiers.

Table 2.7 Variable Modifiers

Modifier	Applied to	Scope	Storage	Explanation
auto	local var.	block	temporary	The auto modifier is implied for local variables.
register	local var.	block	temporary	Modifier suggests that variable be stored in a machine register.
extern	N/A	block	N/A	The extern modifier tells compiler that variable is declared in another file.
static	local var.	block	permanent	Static local variables have the scope of a local variable and the duration of a global variable.
static	global var.	file	permanent	When used with a global variable, static limits the variable's scope to current file.

Volatile Variables

Another keyword often used when declaring variables is volatile. This modifier tells the compiler that the value of the variable may be changed by a hardware device or a background routine. Therefore, the compiler does not attempt to optimize your program and keeps a copy of the variable's value in a register.

The following example illustrates the usage of the volatile keyword:

```
/* *********************************************** */
/* VOLATILE.C: Declaring volatile variables...      */
/* *********************************************** */
volatile int vInt;              /* Volatile integer */
const    int cInt = 10;         /* Const integer..  */
volatile const int vcInt = 100; /* Volatile const int*/
```

Tip: Using Volatile and Const

Note that a volatile variable may also be declared as const. In such cases, the compiler will not allow your program to change the value of the variable and will also refrain from assuming its contents.

Arrays

Very often your program may need to store and manipulate a set of values of the same type. Suppose that you have to store the daily temperature for a week. You can use seven integer variables to hold the values. C, however, provides a better method with arrays. An *array* is a group of data items of the same type. The format of an array declaration is as follows:

```
data_type array_name[array_size];
```

You can represent the temperatures using the following declaration:

```
int temperature[7];      //Uninitialized
```

or

```
int temperature[7] = { 78, 79, 90, 99, 86, 75, 81 };
```

To access each element of an array, you use the array name followed by an index in brackets. The following provides an actual program computing the average temperature:

```
/* ************************************************ */
/* ARRAY.C: Sample using an array...                */
/* ************************************************ */
#include <stdio.h>
#define NUMDAYS  7
int main( void )
{
  int temperature[NUMDAYS]= { 78, 79, 90, 99, 86, 75, 81 };
  int indx, sum;
  for( indx=0; indx<NUMDAYS; indx++ )
    printf( "Day %d,  Temperature %d F\n",
                                    indx+1,
                                    temperature[indx]);
  for( indx=0, sum=0;
     indx < sizeof( temperature )/sizeof( temperature[0] );
     indx++ )
  {
    sum += temperature[indx];
  }
  printf( "Average temperature %d F\n", sum/NUMDAYS );
  return 0;
}
```

You can make an array multidimensional by declaring multiple bracketed array sizes. Two-dimensional arrays are commonly used to represent matrices, 2-D coordinates, and checker boards.

Pointers

A *pointer* is a variable that holds the address of other variables or functions. The declaration of a pointer specifies the data type to which the pointer points. The format of a pointer declaration is as follows:

```
type_pointed_to *pointer_name;
```

The following are some pointer declarations:

```
int      *int_ptr;  /* pointer to integer  */
double   *dbl_ptr;  /* pointer to double   */
```

To access the object pointed to by the pointer, use the pointer name preceded by an asterisk. For example, *dbl_ptr refers to the double pointed to by dbl_ptr.

The following code illustrates the use of pointers:

```
/* ********************************************** */
/* POINTER.C: Illustrates use of pointer...        */
/* ********************************************** */
#include <stdio.h>
#include <stdlib.h>
int main( void )
{
  int i1 = 100;
  /*
```

```c
     * Declare a pointer which points to integer i1
     */
    int *iptrA = &i1,
        *iptrB;
    /*
     * Show that iptrA points to integer i1
     */
    printf( "Addr. of i1  is %p \n",&i1 );
    printf( "iptrA points to %p \n",iptrA );
    /*
     * By dereferencing the pointer, the value
     * of integer i1 can be obtained
     */
    printf( "Value of i1      = %d \n", i1 );
    printf( "Value of *iptrA  = %d \n",*iptrA );
    /*
     * Using pointer with dynamic memory
     */
    iptrB = malloc( sizeof( int ) );
    /*
     * Assigned the value of i1 to the allocated memory
     */
   *iptrB = i1;
    /*
     * Display the contents of the dynamic memory
     */
    printf( "Value of *iptrB  = %d \n",*iptrB );
    free( iptrB );    /* Cleanup... */
    return 0;
}
```

A pointer of type void can point to an object of any type and it is commonly referred to as a *void pointer*. The malloc function returns a void pointer. This allows the memory returned from malloc to be assigned to pointers of any type.

The following sample illustrates how to use pointers to functions:

```c
/* *********************************************** */
/* PTRFUNC.C: Using pointers to functions...       */
/* *********************************************** */
#include <stdio.h>
int ShowMsg( char *msg )
{
    return printf( msg );
}
int main( void )
{
    /* Declare pointer to function...   */
    int (*ptrFunc)( char* );
    /* Initialize pointer to function.. */
    ptrFunc = ShowMsg;
    /* Call function via pointer...     */
    (*ptrFunc)( "Hello! \n" );
    return 0;
}
```

Array-Pointer Relationship

In C, arrays and pointers are closely related. The name of an array is the address of the first element in the array. So a pointer to the first element of an array can be assigned the name of the array.

```
int  iarray[10];
int *iptr = iarray; /* Similar to iptr = &iarray[0] */
```

C also supports incrementing and decrementing of pointers. Incrementing iptr by three(&array[3]) makes the pointer point to the fourth element of iarray. In other words, each time you increment a pointer, you are actually incrementing the address it points to by the size of its related data type. Because they don't have any related data type, void pointers cannot be used in pointer arithmetic.

A pointer can be subscripted just like an array. The compiler internally converts array subscripting in terms of pointer arithmetic. For example,

```
iarray[3] = 10;
```

is represented as

```
*( iarray + 3 ) = 10;
```

The following example illustrates the relationship of pointers and arrays:

```
/* ************************************************** */
/* PTRARRAY.C: Ilustrates pointer/array relationship */
/* ************************************************** */
#include <stdio.h>
#include <stdlib.h>
#define NUM_ELEMENTS 10
int main( void )
{
    int  iarray[NUM_ELEMENTS];
    int *iptr;
    int indx;
    /* Use subscript with array variable */
    for ( indx=0; indx<NUM_ELEMENTS; indx++ )
        iarray[indx] = indx*10;
    /* Use pointer arithmetic with array */
    for( indx=0; indx<NUM_ELEMENTS; indx++ )
        printf( "At indx %d = %d\n", indx,
                                    *(iarray + indx ) );
    /* Assign pointer addr of array      */
    iptr = iarray;
    /* Use subscript with pointer var.   */
    for( indx=0; indx<NUM_ELEMENTS; indx++ )
        printf( "At indx %d = %d\n", indx, iptr[indx] );
    return 0;
}
```

User-Defined Types

The basic C data types, along with arrays and pointers, provide the building blocks to process real-life data, but they are still far from representing some of the complex information clusters you may have to process. An accounting program may need a data type representing a business transaction. A scientific program may need a data type representing temperature and pressure at a given time. C allows you to define or create data types.

Redefining Data Types

You can use the typedef keyword to assign a new name to a data type. Newly defined types can be used to enhance your program's readability. The syntax for using typedef is as follows:

```
typedef <type> <new_type_name>
```

or

```
typedef <type> <new_type_name>[array_size][...]
```

The following sample defines two new types, Msg and MsgIndx:

```c
/* ************************************************ */
/* TYPEDEF.C: Illustrates usage of 'typedef'         */
/* ************************************************ */
#include <stdio.h>
#include <string.h>
#define MAX_MSG_LEN    100
typedef short MsgIndx;
typedef char  Msg[MAX_MSG_LEN];
int main( void )
{
    MsgIndx indx;
    /* Create array of  Msg     */
    Msg _msgs[3];
    /* Initialize messages      */
    strcpy( _msgs[0], "Hello!\n" );
    strcpy( _msgs[1], "C is fun!\n");
    strcpy( _msgs[2], "Goodbye!\n");
    /* Show messages            */
    for( indx=0;
         indx<sizeof( _msgs )/sizeof( _msgs[0] );
         indx++ )
    {
        printf( _msgs[indx] );
    }
    return 0;
}
```

Enumerated Types

An enumeration type is a set of integers defined with the keyword enum. Each integer is represented by a name. The syntax for defining an enumerated type is as follows:

```
enum type_name { constant_name [= int_value], ... };
```

The integer value is optional and defaults to zero for the first enumerator. Subsequent enumeration constants missing the integer value default to the value of the prior constant plus 1.

For example,

```
enum Computer_Drives{ floppy =1,
        harddrives=2,
        cd_rom=4,
        tape_backup=8};
```

or

```
enum Seasons {Fall, Winter, Spring, Summer};
```

Variables of the enumerated type can be declared using the enum and the type_name followed by the variable name, as follows:

```
enum Computer_Drives  drvA, drvB, drvC;
```

You may decide to use the typedef keyword to assign a shorter type name to enumerated types:

```
/* ************************************************** */
/* ENUM.C: Sample creating and using enum. types...  */
/* ************************************************** */
enum Chess_Pieces {
                    King, Queen, Rook,
                    Bishop, Knight, Pawn
                };
typedef enum Chess_Pieces Piece;
#define NUM_ROW_COL    8
typedef short Board[NUM_ROW_COL][NUM_ROW_COL];
int main( void )
{
```

```
    Board brd;
    brd[0][0] = Rook;
    /*
    etc etc
    */
    return 0;
}
```

Structures

Unlike arrays or enumerated data types, structures allow you to logically
group variables of different data types into new types. The following
structure, for example, could be used to store information about
customers:

```
struct customer_information
{
    char lastName[25];
    char firstName[25];
    char midInitial;
    char address[80];
    char city[25];
    char state[2];
    char zipCode[10];
    long accntNum;
};
```

As with other types, structures can be given another name with the typedef keyword. To access a member of a structure, use the structure instance name followed by a period and the member name. When using a pointer to the structure, replace the period with ->. The following example uses a simplified customer_information structure:

```c
/* ********************************************* */
/* STRUCT.C: Using structures...                 */
/* ********************************************* */
#include <stdio.h>
#include <string.h>
typedef struct
{
    char Name[80];
    long accntNum;
}   custInfo;
int main( void )
{
    custInfo newCust;
    strcpy( newCust.Name, "Jean-Claude Payette" );
    newCust.accntNum = 100;
    printf( "New customer information.\n" );
    printf( "Name: %s \n", newCust.Name );
    printf( "Acct: %ld\n", newCust.accntNum );
    return 0;
}
```

Unions

Unions are similar to structures except that all the members share the same memory space. The compiler allocates enough space for the largest union data member. For example, an instance of the following union

```
    union payment
    {
        char poNumber[25];
        char creditCrd[25];
        long chkNumber;
    };
```

causes the compiler to set aside room for just an array of 25 characters.
It is common to embed a union in a structure, because an extra structure
member can be used to help identify which section of the union is
relevant. Following is an example using this union:

```
/* ************************************************ */
/* UNION.C : Using Unions...                        */
/* ************************************************ */
#include <stdio.h>
#include <string.h>
typedef enum payment_type { PO, CC, CHK } pmntType;
struct  transaction
{
    pmntType pType;             /* Method of payment... */
    union                       /* Payment information  */
    {
        char poNumber[25];
        char creditCrd[25];
        long chkNumber;
    } Info;
};
typedef struct transaction SalesRec;
void ShowSalesInfo( SalesRec s )
{
    switch( s.pType )
    {
```

Lean and Mean Borland C++

```c
        case PO:
            printf( "P.O.  sale : %s\n", s.Info.poNumber );
            break;
        case CC:
            printf( "Credit Card: %s\n", s.Info.creditCrd );
            break;
        case CHK:
            printf( "Check sale : %ld\n", s.Info.chkNumber );
            break;
    }
}
int main( void )
{
    SalesRec s1, s2;
    s1.pType    = PO;
    strcpy( s1.Info.poNumber, "#PFT-34982-56" );
    s2.pType    = CHK;
    s2.Info.chkNumber= 34763L;
    ShowSalesInfo( s1 );
    ShowSalesInfo( s2 );
    return 0;
}
```

Bit Fields

Bit fields are structure members with a specified width in bits. This
feature of C allows you to pack the members of a structure. Suppose that
you need to represent the current time with a structure. The following
sample illustrates two data types that can be used:

```
struct simpleTime
{
    unsigned tm_min;              /* Minutes 0-59    */
    unsigned tm_hr ;              /* Hours           */
    unsigned isAM  ;              /* AM (PM) flag     */
};
struct simpleTimeBF
{
    unsigned tm_min : 6;          /* Minutes 0-59    */
    unsigned        : 2;          /* Unused padding  */
    unsigned tm_hr  : 4;          /* Hours           */
    unsigned isAM   : 1;          /* AM (PM) flag     */
    unsigned        : 3;          /* Unused padding  */
};
```

The second structure uses bit fields and requires three times less space than the first because it occupies only 16 bits.

Summary

You are now familiar with the usage of 32 keywords of ANSI C: auto, break, case, char, const, continue, default, do, double, else, enum, extern, float, for, goto, if, int, long, register, return, short, signed, sizeof, static, struct, switch, typedef, union, unsigned, void, volatile, and while.

As you learn in the following chapters, Borland C++ provides several extensions to the ANSI standard. If you are writing code that you plan to port to other non-PC environments, you probably will want to avoid extensions or localize them to a few sections.

In the next chapter, you learn about various ANSI C directives that guide the compiler during the first phase of code translation, commonly referred to at the preprocessing phase.

Chapter 3
Preprocessor Directives

Preprocessor directives begin with a **#** and are acted upon by the compiler during the first phase of the compilation process. Unlike earlier compilers, Borland C++ does not generate an intermediate file after evaluating preprocessor directives. A separate utility, however, CPP.EXE, can be used to produce a file after all the directives have been processed. This chapter examines the preprocessor directives and the macros predefined by the compiler. Proper use of preprocessor directives can make your code more robust, portable, and legible. A section at the end of the chapter is devoted to the common usage of preprocessor directives.

Macros: #define

You can use the *#define* directive to associate a name or identifier to a token or sequence of tokens. Identifiers that represent constants often are referred to as *manifest constants* or *symbolic constants*. Identifiers that represent statements are called *macros*. The term *macro*, however, is often used for manifest or symbolic constants. Macros may accept parameters. The following example shows some macros:

```
/* ************************************************* */
/* MACRO.C: Illustrates the '#define' directive...   */
/* ************************************************* */

#include <stdio.h>

/* A Simple Macro.. */
#define PIE             3.14159

/* Macro taking arguments.. */
#define SQR(v)          ( (v) * (v) )
#define AREA( r, a )    ( 0.5 * SQR(r) * (a) )


int main( void )
{
  double angle = 15;
  double radius  = 321;

  angle = angle * PIE/180;  /* Convert degrees to radians */
  printf( "Area of sector: %lf \n", AREA( radius, angle ) );

  return 0;
}
```

Nesting Macros

As shown in the preceding example, macros can be nested. After each expansion, the result is rescanned for possible macro identifiers that are further expanded. An exception is when a macro expansion contains the macro's own identifier name or when a macro expands to a preprocessing directive.

Line Continuation Character

You can use a backslash (\) as a line continuation character for long macros that require multiple lines, as shown:

```c
#include <stdio.h>
#include <stdlib.h>

#define  ERROR( msg )   printf( "ERROR: " msg "\n" );  \
                        abort();

int main( void )
{
    ERROR( "Unable to start application..." );
    return 0;
}
```

Undefining a Macro

A macro can be undefined by using the *#undef* directive. References to the macro identifier after it is undefined result in a compiler error.

Compiler Settings

Borland C++ allows a simple macro to be defined with the -*D* command line option or from the Options|Project|Compiler|Defines settings. Figure 3.1 shows the PIE macro used in the preceding example as now defined in the IDE.

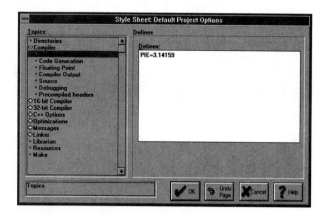

Figure 3.1. *Defining macros in the IDE.*

Command-line users can define the PIE macro using the following option when calling the compiler:

```
BCC -DPIE=3.14159 MACRO.C
```

Command-line users also can undefine a macro using the -*U* option. The IDE does not provide this facility.

Stringizing (#)

The **#** operator can precede a macro argument to instruct the compiler to convert the argument to a string after expansion. As with strings in general, the resulting string is concatenated with adjacent strings if separated by white space only.

Stringizing is commonly used for debugging purposes. The following code, for example, uses two macros that allow the contents of variables to be easily monitored:

```
/* *************************************************** */
/* STRINGIZ.C: Using the # operator in macros...     */
/* *************************************************** */
#include <stdio.h>

#define SHOWINTVAR(var) printf( #var "= %d \n", (int)(var) )
#define SHOWDBLVAR(var) printf( #var "= %lf\n",
(double)(var) )


int main( void )
{
    int    counter = 10;
    double current = 300.1459;

    SHOWINTVAR( counter );
    SHOWDBLVAR( current );

    return 0;
}
```

Token Pasting (##)

The *Token Pasting* operator, ##, combines two tokens on each side of the operator. The new token is then rescanned for possible macro expansion. The following example combines the # and ## operators to provide macros that manage variable names:

```
/* ************************************************ */
/* TOKNPSTE.C: Using the ## operator...            */
/* ************************************************ */
#include <stdio.h>

#define DEF_VARi( n )  int __var_ ## n
#define USE_VARi( n )      __var_ ## n
#define SHW_VARi( n )  printf( "__var_" #n " = %d\n", \
                               __var_ ## n )

int main( void )
{
  DEF_VARi( 1a );        /* Expands to 'int __var_1a;'  */
  DEF_VARi( 1b );        /* Expands to 'int __var_1b;'  */

  USE_VARi( 1a ) = 10;  /* Expands to '__var_1a = 10;'  */
  USE_VARi( 1b ) = 20;  /* Expands to '__var_1b = 20;'  */

  SHW_VARi( 1a ); /*printf( "__var_1a = %d\n", __var_1a );*/
  SHW_VARi( 1b ); /*printf( "__var_1b = %d\n", __var_1b );*/

  return 0;
}
```

Macro Caveats

Macros often simplify tasks by assigning a single identifier to a series of statements. They also make code more readable because the macro name often clarifies the statements or value represented. However, macros have the following disadvantages:

- Macros are not type-safe. In other words, there is no built-in mechanism in the compiler to ensure that you pass the proper type of arguments to a macro.

- Macros may produce side effects if an argument is evaluated more than once. The following macros defined in the *STDLIB.H* header file, for example, must be used with caution:

```
#define max(a,b)    (((a) > (b)) ? (a) : (b))
#define min(a,b)    (((a) < (b)) ? (a) : (b))
```

The following example shows the side effect of the *min* and *max* macros:

```
/* ************************************************ */
/* MIN_MAX.C: Illustrates macro side effects...      */
/* ************************************************ */

#include <stdlib.h>
#include <stdio.h>


int main( void )
{
    int i=10;
    int j=14;
    int mx, mn;

    printf( "Values before macro: i= %d,  j= %d \n", i, j );

    mx = max( i++, j-- );
    mn = min( i++, j-- );
```

```
    printf( "Values after  macro: i= %d,  j= %d \n", i, j );

    return 0;
}
```

Figure 3.2 shows the output of the *min_max* program:

Figure 3.2. *Output of min_max.exe.*

The *min_max* code only decremented i twice; however, its final value is three units less than the original! Similarly, the final value of j is three units more than the original although it was incremented only twice.

The #include Directive

You've seen the *#include* directive used in the various samples provided so far. The #include directive instructs the compiler to insert the contents of another file at the location of the directive. It is commonly used for header files or include files; however, you also may include another source file within your program source. Include files usually contain type definitions, declarations of external variables, macros, and C++ inline functions which are shared by more than one module. The #include syntax is

```
#include <filename>
#include "filename"
```

If *filename* is not a fully qualified filename, only the specified *include directories* are searched in the first form. In the second form, the current directory is searched first followed by the specified *include directories*.

Conditional Compilation

You can selectively compile sections of a file by evaluating a constant expression or identifier. The directives *#if, #elif, #else,* and *#endif* are provided for that purpose. The syntax is as follows:

```
#if        expression_1

    // Compiled if expression_1 is true

#elseif expression_2

    // Compiled if expression_2 is true and...
    // expression_1 is *NOT* true!!

#elseif expression_3

    // Compiled if expression_1 and expression_2 are
    // not true and expression_3 is true!!
#else

    // Compiled if all expressions are false

#endif
```

The following rules apply to the use of *#if/#elif/#else* and *#endif*:

- For every *#if* there must be a matching *#endif* directive.

- The *#elif* and *#else* directives are optional.

- While there may be any number of *#elif* between the *#if* and *#endif*, only one *#else* directive is allowed, and it must precede the *#endif* statement.

- Similar to the C *if/else* statements, the section following the first true expression is compiled.

- If none of the expressions are true, the section following the optional *#else* is compiled.

- The expression must evaluate to an integer constant and cannot use the *sizeof* operator.

Using Operators with Preprocessor Conditional Expressions

The expression can use the **==**, **>**, **>=**, **<**, and **<=** operators. For example, Windows programmers often evaluate the symbol *WINVER* which is defined as 0x0300 and 0x030a for Windows v3.0 and 3.1 respectively, as shown:

```
/* ************************************************** */
/* WIN3031.C: Using preprocessor to evaluate WINVER. */
/* ************************************************** */

#include <windows.h>

#if (WINVER < 0x030a)       /* v3.0 WINDOWS.H compatible!! */
    typedef WORD    WINMSG;
#else                       /* v3.1 and above....          */
    typedef UINT    WINMSG;
#endif
```

The defined Operator

The operator *defined* can be used with either the #*if* or #*elif* directives. It allows you to test whether an identifier or macro has been defined. The following code illustrates:

```
void ShowMessage( char *msg )
{

#if defined(DOS_TARGET)
    puts( msg );
#else
    MessageBox( NULL, msg, "MSG", MB_OK|MB_TASKMODAL );
#endif

}
```

If the macro DOS_TARGET is defined, the function *ShowMessage( )* uses the *puts* function to display the message. Otherwise, the MessageBox( ) function is used.

You can combine the logical negation '!' operator to check whether an identifier is not currently defined. Hence the *ShowMessage( )* function could be rewritten as:

```
void ShowMessage( char *msg )
{

#if !defined(DOS_TARGET)
    MessageBox( NULL, msg, "MSG", MB_OK|MB_TASKMODAL );
#else
    puts( msg );
#endif

}
```

#ifdef and #ifndef

The *#ifdef* and *#ifndef* directives are equivalent to the *#if defined* and *#if !defined* directives. They allow you to check whether an identifier is currently defined or not. The *defined* operator is preferred to the *#ifdef/#ifndef* directive because it allows the testing of multiple macros via complex logical expressions, as shown:

```
#ifdef      DOSTARGET
    #ifndef NDEBUG
            puts( msg );
    #endif
#endif
```

can be simplified to

```
#if defined(DOSTARGET) && !defined(NDEBUG)
    puts( dbgmsg );
#endif
```

The #error Directive

The error directive produces a compile-time error message. The syntax is the following:

```
    #error   Error_Message
```

Error_Message can include macro identifiers that are expanded by the preprocessor. The directive commonly is used when a required identifier has not been defined, as shown:

```
/* ************************************************ */
/* ERROR.C: Using #error...                         */
/* ************************************************ */
```

```
/* Check the target environment... */

#if !defined(DOS)  && !defined(WINDOWS)
#error You must define either DOS or WINDOWS
#endif

#if defined(DOS)    &&  defined(WINDOWS)
#error You cannot defined both DOS and WINDOWS
#endif
```

The #line Directive

The *#line* directive can be used to adjust the internal line number count of the compiler. The *#line* directive has the following syntax:

```
#line      line_num ["filename"]
```

line_num must be an integer constant. An optional *filename* also can be specified. This directive alters the predefined __LINE__ macro. If a *filename* is specified, the __FILE__ macro also is modified.

The #pragma Directive

The *#pragma* directive allows a C/C++ compiler to support features specific to the compiler. The syntax is as follows:

```
#pragma pragma_directive
```

Table 3.1 describes the pragma directives supported by the Borland C++ compiler.

Table 3.1 Borland C++ Pragma Directives

Directive	Description
argsused:	Disables the warning message Parameter *xxxx* is never used in function *ffff* for the function following the pragma.
exit:	Allows you to specify a function that is called just before the program terminates. The syntax is as follows: #pragma exit *functionName* [*priority*]
extref:	Allows you to force the compiler to include a reference to an unused external variable or function, as shown in the code that follows this table:
hdrfile:	Specifies the name of the precompiled header file.
hdrignore:	Because the macros and types declared in a header file may change when another macro is defined, the compiler refrains from using the information in a precompiled header file upon encountering conditional compilation directives. You can instruct the compiler to use the precompiled header in spite of conditional compilation depending on an identifier. The syntax is #pragma hdrignore *identifier* *identifier* refers to the symbol that is evaluated in a preprocessor conditional statement.
hdrstop:	Informs the compiler not to include any more information in the precompiled header file.
inline:	Informs the compiler to compile the current translation unit via assembly. In other words, the compiler generates assembler code from your C/C++ module and then calls TASM (or another specified assembler), which produces the .OBJ file.

Directive	Description
intrinsic:	This option can be used to enable or disable the inline expansion of an intrinsic function. An intrinsic function is a library routine for which the compiler can generate code inline. The syntax is

#pragma intrinsic [-]*funcName*

If the - precedes the function name, the function calls are not expanded inline. The following functions are known to Borland C++:

memchr	memcmp	memcpy	memset
strcat	strchr		
strcmp	strncpy	strnset	
strrchr	strset	rotl	
rotr	fabs	alloca	

obsolete:	The obsolete pragma has the following syntax:

#pragma obsolete *funcName*

This causes the compiler to generate the message `Warning` *filename linenum*: `'funcName' is obsolete in function xxxx`. It can be used to warn other programmers that you have enhanced your code and have provided a newer function for a particular task.

option:	The option pragma allows you to include command-line options into your code. Some command-line options may not be used with this pragma. Some options must appear at the top of your source code. Use this option when you absolutely need to ensure that some settings are used when compiling a particular module.

continues

Table 3.1 continued

Directive	Description
startup:	This pragma is the counterpart of the exit pragma. It allows you to specify a function that is executed before the function *main*, *WinMain*, *LibMain*, or *DLLEntryPoint* is called.
warn:	The warn pragma allows you to customize the warnings enabled or disabled within your source code. The syntax is #pragma warn +l-l.*xxx* where '*xxx*' represents a particular warning. If the + precedes the symbol, the warning is enabled. A leading – disables the warning, and a leading . restores the setting of that warning to its original state.

Using #pragma Option with the RTL Source

Sometimes it is useful to include one or more files from the Borland Runtime Library to your own project to debug a failing application. Because the runtime library is built with specific compiler settings, you can insert the following *#pragma option* line at the top of the RTL source to ensure that your compiler settings do not conflict with the ones required for the RTL sources:

```
#pragma option -a- -k- -zC_TEXT -zR_DATA -zTDATA
```

```
/* ************************************************ */
/* EXTREF.C: Illustrates the #pragma extref...      */
/* ************************************************ */

#include <stdio.h>

extern int unusedInt1;
extern int unusedInt2;

void funcNotCalled1( void );
void funcNotCalled2( void );

#pragma extref unusedInt2
#pragma extref funcNotCalled2


int main( void )
{
    printf( "Hello, world \n" );
    return 0;
}
```

The compiler inserts a record in the resulting .OBJ file indicating that the external function *printf* is used. Normally, these records are not generated for external variables or functions that are declared but never used within the translation unit. With the pragma *extref*, you can force the compiler to generate the external definition record (commonly referred to as EXTDEF) for unused external variables and functions. The .OBJ generated for the preceding sample contains EXTDEFs for the variable 'unusedInt2' and the function 'funcNotCalled2'.

Predefined Macros

The compiler automatically defines some macros.

ANSI Macros

Table 3.2 describes the ANSI macros automatically defined by the compiler.

Table 3.2 Predefined ANSI Macros

Macro	Description
__DATE__:	String in the form *mmm dd yyyy* representing the date the current file was preprocessed.
__FILE__:	String of name of current source file with double quotation marks.[NOTE: #*line* directive may change the meaning of __FILE__.]
__LINE__:	Integer representing the line number in the current source file. [NOTE: #*line* directive may change the meaning of __LINE__.]
__STDC__:	Evaluates to the integer constant 1 when the ANSI Compatibility option is enabled [-**A** on for BCC, BCC32, and Options I Project I Compiler I Source I Language_Compliance I ANSI from the IDE]. Otherwise, the macro is not defined.
__TIME__:	String in the form *hh:mm:ss* representing the time the current file was preprocessed.

The following program shows common usage of the preceding macros:

```
/* ************************************************** */
/* ANSIMAC.C: Using the Predefined ANSI macros...        */
/* ************************************************** */

#include  <stdio.h>

char  buildDate[]  =  __DATE__;
char  buildTime[]  =  __TIME__;


int  main( void )
{
   FILE  *fp;

   printf(  SMPL  Version  2.01  Copyright  (c)  1994
                 A.B.  co.  Ltd\n);
   printf(  Built  on  %s  @  %s  \n,  buildDate,  buildTime );

   if  (  (fp = fopen(  \\FILE\\SAMPLE.NOT ,  r+t  ))  ==  NULL)
   {
      printf(  fopen()  error  in  %s  at  line  %d  \n,  __FILE__,
                                               __LINE__);

      return 0;
   }
   /*
    ...
   */
   return 0;
}
```

Borland C++ Macros

Besides the ANSI macros, Borland C++ also predefines several other identifiers. Table 3.3 describes these macros.

Table 3.3 Borland C++ Macros

Macro	Description
__cplusplus	Defined when the compiler is in C++ mode
__Windows	Defined when compiling 16-bit Windows code or 32-bit NT console or GUI code
__BCPLUSPLUS__	Evaluates to 0x320 when the compiler is in C++ mode
__BORLANDC__	Evaluates to 0x400
__CDECL__	Evaluates to 0x1 if the C calling convention (default) is being used
__CONSOLE__	Defined when compiling a 32-bit Console application
__DLL__	Defined when compiling a 16-bit or 32-bit DLL
__FASTCALL__	Defined when the Register calling convention is being used
__FLAT__	Defined when building a 32-bit application
__MSDOS__	Defined when building a 16-bit application
__MT__	Defined when the multi-thread option is enabled with the 32-bit compiler
__OVERLAY__	Defined when overlays are enabled at compile time (for example, **-Y** when calling BCC.EXE)

Macro	Description
__PASCAL__	Defined when the Pascal calling convention is enabled
__TCPLUSPLUS__	Defined when the compiler is in C++ mode (similar to __BCPLUSPLUS__)
__TEMPLATES__	Indicates that Borland C++ supports templates
__TLS__	Defined for the 32-bit compiler for both GUI and console applications
__TURBOC__	Evaluates to 0x400 (similar to __BORLANDC__)
__WIN32__	Defined when using the 32-bit compiler for both GUI and console applications

When compiling 16-bit applications, Borland C++ also defines one of the following macros to indicate the memory model in use: __TINY__, __SMALL__, __MEDIUM__, __COMPACT__, __LARGE__, __HUGE__.

Common Use of Preprocessor Directives

Now that you've seen the various preprocessor directives, let's look at some of their common applications.

Preventing Multiple Inclusion of Header Files

You can prevent multiple inclusion of header files with the use of a sentry. The following sample header file illustrates:

```
#if !defined(__SAMPLE_H)
#define      __SAMPLE_H

    //
    // Declarations, macros,
    // type definitions etc.
    // go here...
    //

#endif  //    __SAMPLE_H
```

The preceding code ensures that only one copy of the header file is included even if the file is indirectly included more than once in the current translation unit.

Easily Commenting Out Sections of Code

It is very common to use an *#if 0/endif pair* to comment out a section of code. Actually, a combination of the *#if 0/#else/endif* directives allows you to easily switch between two sets of code. This technique can be very useful while experimenting. The following code shows this point:

```
/* ********************************************** */
/* IF_0_1.C: Using #if to easily comment out code... */
/* ********************************************** */
```

```
void SortData()
{
#if 0    // Change to '1' to use faster algorithm when
         // Bruneau fixes crash bug.           (Bill)
    //
    //  Code of fast algorithm goes here
    //
#else
    //
    //  Code of slower algorithm goes here
    //
#endif
}
```

Ensuring Proper Compiler Settings

It is a good idea to verify that your code is always compiled with the proper settings. By checking for the various macros predefined by the compiler, you can catch several types of improper settings. The following sample illustrates some of the macros frequently used for that purpose.

```
////////////////////////////////////////////////////
// MAC_CHK.CPP: Using macros to verify proper settings/
////////////////////////////////////////////////////

#if !defined(__cplusplus)
#error  This file must be compiled in C++ mode
#endif

#if !defined(__Windows)
#error  This file can only be used in Windows Applications
#endif
```

```
#if !defined(__WIN32__)
#error  This file uses VBXs and does not support Win32
#endif

#if !defined(__COMPACT__) && !defined(__LARGE__)
#error  This file requires far data pointers
#endif
```

Diagnostic Macros

You can use the **#** operator to simplify macros that display diagnostic messages. Various diagnostic macros also combine the __FILE__ and __LINE__ identifiers to enhance error reporting mechanisms. The following example illustrates two macros that make use of the preprocessor.

```
#include <stdio.h>

#define INFO(msg) printf( "INFO: " #msg "\n" )
#define WARN(msg) printf( "WARN: " #msg " (" __FILE__ ")" \
                          " at line %d \n ", __LINE__  )

int main( void )
{
    INFO( Entering main );

    //
    // Try something that fails!
    WARN( call to xxxx failed );

    return 0;
}
```

Summary

With the advent of C++, programmers rely less and less on preprocessor macros (C++ constants, inline functions, and templates offer better alternatives). However, preprocessor directives are still invaluable and, as shown in the code of this chapter, provide the means to make your code more robust, readable, and portable.

Chapter 4
The C Language Extensions

In the ideal world, a high-level language such as C would completely conceal the specific aspects of a CPU and Operating System while taking full advantage of their features. You could write portable ANSI code that could be easily recompiled with other compilers or even ported to another architecture. However, this ideal world is only achievable for applications requiring minimal user interaction and system resources. To allow full access to an environment's features or to work around any of the environment's limitations, compilers offer language extensions. This chapter introduces you to the Borland C++ extensions aimed at taking advantage of the features of the INTEL 80x86 CPUs. For the most part, this chapter covers issues that are specific to the 16-bit DOS and Windows environments. The extensions provided by Borland C++ are in the form of new keywords and compiler settings.

Segments

Most of you have a few megabytes of RAM on your machines and you think of that memory as ranging from 0 through xMBs. In other words, you think of the memory in a linear fashion. From a programming perspective, the 80x86 CPU does not address memory in a linear way but rather in terms of segments. A *segment* is a chunk of memory starting at a linear address divisible by 16. Each segment is 64K in length. To reference a memory location, you must specify a segment value plus an offset within the segment. Actually, the segment value is first loaded in a segment register and then the processor is requested to perform some operation at an offset within the segment. The CPU contains four basic *segment registers* that can be used for accessing memory in the following ways:

- CS (code segment). The CS register holds the segment of all executable instructions or functions.

- DS (data segment). The DS register contains the default segment value for accessing global and static variables.

- SS (stack segment). The SS register holds the segment of the program's stack where the space for local variables is allocated.

- ES (extra segment). The ES register is an additional segment register commonly used when accessing global and static variables.

When accessing memory, the CPU internally combines the value of a segment register and the specified offset to compute the linear address being referred to. This quick description of the CPU's addressing mode is applicable to the DOS environment but is slightly different under Windows 16-bit. Under Windows 16-bit, the segment does not contain the real address of a chunk of memory; instead, it is an index (or *selector*) into a table (*descriptor table*) where that address is stored. Nevertheless, under both environments, an address is comprised of a segment:offset pair. You can think of a function name as being the offset of a unit of code within a particular code segment. Similarly, a variable name is just an offset within a segment where the compiler has set aside some space.

To access a variable, the DS register is first loaded with the proper base value and then an offset is specified to the CPU. Similarly, when calling a function, the CPU may need to load a new segment value prior to transferring control to the offset of the function. Each time a new segment is specified, there is a small overhead involved because a segment register must be reloaded with a new value. Ideally, all of your program's data would fit in the same segment with each variable distinguishable solely by its offset within the segment. This would eliminate the need to reload the DS register. Likewise, having all of your program's code in one segment, with each function at a unique offset would eliminate the need to constantly update the CS register. However, because each segment only can be up to 64K in length, this would limit you to 64K of code or data! This limitation was acceptable a few years ago, but nowadays it is not uncommon for applications to occupy megabytes of memory. To allow easy selection and permutation between better performance with one segment or the larger capacities of code or data with multiple segments, Borland C++ provides memory models.

Memory Models

Memory models are compiler settings governing the resources set aside for your application. A DOS application must be compiled using one of the six available memory models (Tiny, Small, Medium, Compact, Large, and Huge). Windows applications only have four possible memory models: Small, Medium, Compact, and Large. Besides specifying your program's code and data requirements, the memory model you choose also affects the size of your generic pointers, the amount of default heap, and, in the case of DOS applications, the size of the application's stack. Table 4.1 outlines the attributes of the six memory models for DOS applications.

Table 4.1 DOS Memory Models

Model	*Code*	*Data*	*Stack*	*Default Heap & Data Ptr.*
Tiny	Code +	Data +	Stack+Heap up to 64K	(near)
Small	64K	Data +	Stack+Heap up to 64K	(near)
Medium	64K/file	Data +	Stack+Heap up to 64K	(near)
Compact	64K	64K	64K	far
Large	64K/file	64K	64K	far
Huge	64K/file	64K/file	64K	far

Tables 4.2 and 4.3 outline the attributes of the four memory models available for Windows executables and DLLs.

Table 4.2 Windows (EXE) Memory Models

Model	Code	Data	Stack	Default Heap & Data Ptr.
Small	64K	Data +	Stack+Heap up to 64K	(near)
Medium	64K/file	Data +	Stack+Heap up to 64K	(near)
Compact	64K	Data +	Stack up to 64K	far
Large	64K/file	Data +	Stack up to 64K	far

Table 4.3 Windows (DLL) Memory Models

Model	Code	Data	Stack	Default Heap & Data Ptr.
Small	64K	~64K	N/A	far
Medium	64K/file	~64K	N/A	far
Compact	64K	~64K	N/A	far
Large	64K/file	~64K	N/A	far

Near and Far Pointers

Closely related to memory models are the sizes of code and data pointers. A *near pointer* contains only the offset portion of an address, but the segment half is assumed to be in one of the segment registers of the CPU. Models with a near heap (tiny, small, and medium) default to near data pointers and usually assume the value of the DS register as the segment for the pointers. Models that do not support more than 64K of code (tiny, small, and compact) default to near function or code pointers. The segment portion of the address is the value in the CS register.

Far pointers contain both the segment and offset portion of an address. The compact, large and huge memory models use far data pointers and the medium, large and huge memory models default to far function pointers. Regardless of the memory model; however, you can use the keywords _ _**near** or _ _**far** if you want to override the size of a pointer. The syntax is

```
type __near *variable_name;
```

or

```
type __far  *variable_name;
```

Make sure that the keyword _ _near or _ _far precedes the *. When inserted between the * and the variable name, the modifier may change the location of the pointer but will not affect the pointer size. The following example illustrates the size and contents of near and far pointers. You may want to compile and link this example in at least the small and large memory models to notice the difference in default pointer sizes.

```
/* ************************************************* */
/* PTRSIZE.C: Sample illustrating size of pointers.. */
/* ************************************************* */

#include <stdio.h>

char     Var[] = "Hello!";


int main( void )
{
  char *p = Var;              /* Generic pointer  */

  char far  *fp = Var;        /* Far pointer....  */
```

```
char near *np = Var;          /* Near pointer...  */

printf( "Global variable is at %p \n", Var );
printf( "Size of generic pointer is %d bytes \n", sizeof( p ) );
printf( "Generic pointer points  to %p \n", p );

printf( "Size of a far  pointer  is %d bytes \n", sizeof( fp ) );
printf( "The far pointer points  to %Fp \n", fp );

printf( "Size of a near pointer  is %d bytes \n", sizeof( np ) );
printf( "The near pointer points to %p \n", np );

return 0;
}
```

Remember that the compiler can always promote a near pointer to a far
pointer. A far pointer cannot, however, be converted to a near pointer.
For example, when compiling the preceding example in a far data model
such as LARGE, you'll notice that the last call to *printf* displays an
invalid address.

Huge Pointers

When performing pointer arithmetic, only the offset portion of a far
pointer is modified. This implies that a far pointer being incremented
may wrap back to offset zero upon reaching the end of a segment. To
cause the compiler to generate code that allows a pointer to step beyond
the current segment, you can use the _ _**huge** modifier when declaring
the pointer. The syntax is similar to that of near or far pointers:

```
type      __huge *pointer_name;
```

The technique used by the compiler differs for the DOS and Windows environment; however, the result is the same—no segment wraparound!

Huge Pointers under DOS

For programs targeting the DOS environment, the compiler will constantly *normalize* the pointer when you increment or decrement its value. In other words, the compiler constantly ensures that the offset portion of the pointer does not exceed 15 (0x0F) bytes by adjusting the segment. The following DOS example illustrates pointer normalization.

```
/* ************************************************ */
/* HPTRDOS.C: Example to show huge ptr normalization.*/
/* ************************************************ */

#include <stdio.h>

int main( void )
{
    long __huge *hp = NULL;

    int count;
    for( count=0; count<10; count++ )
    {
        printf( "hp[%d] is at address %Fp\n", count, &hp[count] );
    }

    for( count=0; count<10; count++ )
    {
        printf( "hp contains address %Fp\n", hp );
        hp++;
    }
}
```

```
    return 0;
}
```

As shown by the example, the compiler also normalizes the resulting address when the code uses the array notation to access the elements pointed to by the huge pointer.

Huge Pointers under Windows

Under the Windows environment, normalization only takes place after the offset wraps back to the beginning of the segment. The following conditions must be met for proper pointer normalization:

- Enable the fast huge pointer option (-h for the command line compiler).

- Perform pointer arithmetic in powers of 2. If your pointer is of a user defined type whose size is not a power of 2, you will need to pad the type with extra bytes. For example, if the variable points to the following type

```
struct  CustInfo
{
    char  lastName[13];
    char  firstName[13];
    long  accountNum;
};

struct CustInfo __huge *pBigCustList;
```

you will need to pad the structure as follows for the pointer to be properly normalized when performing pointer arithmetic:

```
struct  CustInfo
{
```

```
            char   lastName[13];
            char   firstName[13];
            long   accountNum;
            short  _padding_to_make_struct_32_bytes;
       };

       struct CustInfo __huge *pBigCustList;
```

Macros To Manipulate Pointers

The header file *DOS.H* defines three macros that allow easy manipulation of pointers.

- FP_OFF(fp)   This macro returns the offset of a pointer.

- FP_SEG(fp)   This macro returns the segment of a pointer.

- MK_FP(s, o)   This macro returns a far pointer made up of the segment and offset passed as parameters.

It is helpful not to limit the term pointers to pointer variables. For example, FP_OFF and FP_SEG can be used with the address of a variable.

```
/* ************************************************ */
/* PTRMAC.C: Using FP_SEG and FP_OFF macros...      */
/* ************************************************ */

#include <stdio.h>
#include <dos.h>


int main( void )
{
  int i;
```

```
    printf( "Address of local var: %p \n", &i );
    printf( "Address of local val: %04X:%04X \n",
                                    FP_SEG( &i ),
                                    FP_OFF( &i ) );
    return 0;
}
```

Which Segment?

A __near pointer holds only the offset of a pointer. The segment used by
the compiler when the pointer is dereferenced depends on the type of
pointer: near data pointers use the contents of the DS register, and near
function pointers default to CS value. You can, however, change the
default segment register associated with a near pointer by using one of
the following keywords:

- __cs: use CS register with near pointer.

- __ds: use DS register with near pointer.

- __es: use ES register with near pointer.

- __ss: use SS register with near pointer.

In the following example, a DLL accesses the first word of the stack
segment by using the __ss modifier with a near data pointer. This technique is commonly used by DLLs wanting to access variables in an
application since the stack segment of a DLL is actually the data segment
of the application calling into the DLL.

```
#include <windows.h>

short __ss *appTaskHdrPtr;
```

```
void CALLBACK _export DLLFunction( void )
{
    short s1 = *appTaskHdrPtr;
}
```

You can declare a pointer variable that only holds the segment portion of
an address by using the __*seg* modifier. A full pointer can later be ob-
tained by adding the segment pointer variable to a near variable that
contributes the offset portion of the address. In the following example,
the segment of an array of messages is saved in a segment pointer
variable. An offset within the array is later computed based on a message index. The offset and segment are then combined and passed to the
printf function. Because printf is passed a far pointer, this sample must
be compiled in the Compact or Large memory model.

```
/* ************************************************* */
/* SEG.C: Using segment pointer types...            */
/* ************************************************* */

#include <stdio.h>
#include <dos.h>

char *msg[] = { "This is the first message",
                "The next one!",
                "And, the last message"
              };
char __seg *msgSeg;


void ShowMsg( int indx )
{
    char __near *msgOff = ( char __near* )msg[indx];
    printf( msgSeg+msgOff );
}
```

```
int main( void )
{
    /* Initialize segment... */
    msgSeg = ( char __seg* )msg;

    ShowMsg( 1 );

    return 0;
}
```

Variable Modifiers

Tables 4.1, 4.2, and 4.3 indicated that all memory models, except for huge, have only one segment for all the global data of the application. This can be a serious limitation if your program requires large amounts of global and static variables. You can declare variables that are not placed in the default data segment by using the keywords __far or __huge. This is a technique commonly used by applications requiring more than 64K of global or static data.

__far

The __**far** modifier instructs the compiler to place a variable in a far data segment. You must ensure that the modifier precedes the variable name, especially when using pointers. See the following example.

```
/* ************************************************ */
/* FARVAR.C:  Illustrates use of __far modifier...   */
/* ************************************************ */
```

```
/* Variable located in default data segment */
int     i = 0;

/* Variable located in far data segment...  */
int far j = 0;

/* Pointer located in default data segment  */
int     *ip1 =&i;

/* Far pointer in default data segment      */
int far *ip2 =&i;

/* Default pointer in far data segment...    */
int * far ip3=&i;

/* Far pointer in far data segment...        */
int far * far ip4= &i;
```

If, while compiling or linking a program, you receive a message indicating that there is too much global data, identify a few large variables and add the __far modifier when declaring them. For example, the following file generates the Too much global data defined in file error message.

```
/* Sample file with too much global data */

int    intTable1[32000];
int    intTable2[32000];
char   msg[]="Performing computation, please wait!";
long   counter1, counter2;
```

To eliminate the error message, use the __far modifier when declaring the two large arrays.

```
int    __far intTable1[32000];
int    __far intTable2[32000];
char   msg[]="Performing computation, please wait!";
long   counter1, counter2;
```

__huge

The size limitation of segments becomes really obvious when you need to declare a variable that exceeds 64K. For example, the following declaration

```
long   Table[20000];
```

generates the Array size too large error message. The __**huge** modifier can be used to instruct the compiler to set aside two or more segments for a single variable. In other words, a __huge variable is similar to a __far variable, except that the former can exceed 64K in size. As with the __far keyword, make sure that the modifier precedes the variable name as shown below

```
long   __huge Table[20000];
```

Function Modifiers

Just like data pointers, functions and function pointers default to near or far depending on the memory models. Again, you can use the keywords __**near** or __**far** to override the function or function pointer size. For example

```
/* ********************************************** */
/* FARFUNC.C: __far and __near functions & ptrs..    */
/* ********************************************** */
```

```c
#include <stdio.h>

void __far  farFunction( int i )
{
    printf( "farFunction() received %d\n", i );
}


void __near nearFunction( char *msg )
{
    printf( "nearFunction() received %s", msg );
}


/* Declare and initialize near function pointer */
void (__near *nFuncPtr )( char* ) = nearFunction;

/* Declare and initialize far function pointer  */
void (__far  *fFuncPtr )( int    ) = farFunction;


int main( void )
{
    /* Call the functions via function pointers.. */

    fFuncPtr( 10 );
    nFuncPtr( "A Greeting Message!" );
    return 0;
}
```

Functions called by the operating system or by device drivers must be explicitly declared as __far unless you are in a far code memory model. For instance, if you are writing a program for the DOS environment, you can use the mouse API and specify one of your functions to be used as mouse event handler. The function will be called whenever a mouse button is pressed or the mouse is moved. If you are in a memory model with near code (tiny, small, compact), the function handling mouse events must explicitly be declared as __far because they are called from the mouse driver. Windows programs make extensive use of callback functions. These functions are called directly by Windows and must also use the keyword __far or FAR.

__interrupt

Some events cause the CPU to temporarily suspend its current execution and to transfer control to another piece of code. These events are referred to as *interrupts* and can be triggered by either hardware or software. For example, if you use your keyboard while a program is performing a lengthy computation, each keypress results in a temporary transfer to an *interrupt handler* or *interrupt service routine* (ISR) that stores the value of the key pressed in a buffer. If the busy program does not check for keypresses, eventually the keyboard interrupt handler will start beeping, informing you that the buffer is full. Interrupt handlers are usually written in assembly language because it offers better control and avoids the overhead of high level languages. You can, however, write a C function that will service interrupts by using the __**interrupt** modifier. The modifier causes the compiler to generate code that

- saves and restores registers upon entering and exiting the function respectively.

- restores the data segment register with the address of the program's default data segment allowing access to global and static variables from within the handler.

- terminates the function with the *IRET* instruction.

The Borland C++ Library provides the *setvect()* function that can be used to install and activate the routine at runtime. Unless you are writing a *Terminate and Stay Resident* (TSR) application, it is good practice to save the value of the prior handler before installing yours. The *getvect()* library function can be used to retrieve the current handler of an interrupt. Before exiting your application, restore the prior handler. The following examples illustrate the basic steps involved in installing your interrupt service routine.

```
#include <dos.h>

#define INT_NUMBER   0x60

void interrupt ( *oldHandler )( void );


void interrupt newHandler( void )
{
    /* Call the old handler first */
    oldHandler();

    /*
    do some processing before returning...
    */
}


void interrupt AnotherHandler( void )
{
    /*
    do some processing first...
    */

    /* Chain to old handler */
    chain_intr( oldHandler );
}
```

```c
void InstallHandler( void )
{
    /* Save the value of the current handler */
    oldHandler = getvect( INT_NUMBER );

    /* Install our handler.. */
    setvect( newHandler, INT_NUMBER );
}


void RestoreHandler( void )
{
    setvect( oldhandler, INT_NUMBER );
    return 0;
}
```

An interrupt handler may opt to call the original handler before performing any processing. Alternatively, the *chain_intr* function may be used to jump to the old handler. This function does not return to the handler.

__saveregs, __loadds

When generating machine code for your functions, the C compiler follows a set of rules regarding register usage. The code generated saves and restores the contents of some registers if the registers are used within the function. The values of other registers are never preserved. This understanding among functions ensures that important data is only kept in registers that are preserved before calling a routine. It also allows some registers to be freely used without the overhead of saving and restoring their contents. Unfortunately, this rule of register use may not be observed by every routine that calls your code. You may need to interface with a function that has been coded in assembly language or in another high level language with different register usage agreements. Your code may even be called from a device driver or some other applications. For these scenarios, Borland C++ provides the __saveregs and __loadds function modifiers.

The __**saveregs** modifier instructs the compiler to explicitly save the values of all registers before executing the body of the function and to restore them at the end of the function body. Use the __saveregs modifier when interfacing with routines that expect your function to preserve the contents of all registers. __**loadds** directs the compiler to save the current value of the data segment register and reset it to the value of your program's default data segment before executing the body of the function. The original value of the data segment register is restored upon exiting the function. __loadds is useful if your function may be called from a routine that has modified the original value of your DS register.

__export

The __**export** function modifier is somewhat similar to __**loadds** but is specific to programs targeting the Windows 16-bit environment. It instructs the compiler to generate code that allows the function to access your program's global variables when the function is called from another application or from Windows directly. Functions declared with the __**export** modifier must use the far modifier when used in small or medium memory models.

Calling Conventions

The order in which the parameters of a particular function are pushed on the stack and the way they are cleaned up is referred to as the *calling convention*. The convention used by the compiler when calling a function depends on the current compiler calling convention setting and the function declaration. A function may use one of several keywords to indicate the method by which it should be called.

__cdecl

By default the compiler uses the C-calling convention for functions that do not explicitly specify the way they expect parameters. However, you can configure the compiler to use a different default calling convention. Hence, several libraries explicitly request the C calling convention by using the __**cdecl** function modifier. For example:

```
void   __cdecl  DisplayError( int ErrCode );
```

The __**cdecl** keyword also affects the internal name assigned to the function by the compiler. It instructs the compiler to use the default C-style naming convention, which maintains a case-sensitive copy of the name you specified with an added leading underscore. The internal name of our DisplayError function, therefore, is _DisplayError_.

Although the C calling convention is the default, you can ensure that it is enabled by

- using the -p- or -pc compiler command line option

or

- selecting C from the Project Options dialog, 16-bit Compiler, or 32-bit Compiler Topic and Calling Convention subtopic.

__pascal

With the Pascal-style, parameters are passed in the reverse fashion; they are pushed from right to left. Furthermore the function called is responsible for cleaning the stack. The Pascal calling convention can be more efficient, especially when a function taking parameters is called many times and from several locations. A function using the Pascal-style, however, cannot be declared to expect a variable argument list. To use the Pascal-style, use the __**pascal** function modifier when declaring the function.

```
void __pascal DisplayErrorP( int ErrCode );
```

With the Pascal style, the internal name assigned to the function is similar to the name of your function except that every letter is converted to uppercase. The internal name of the DisplayErrorP function, therefore, is *DISPLAYERRORP*.

You can enable the Pascal-style by

- using the -p compiler command line option

or

- selecting pascal from the Project_Options dialog, 16-bit Compiler, or 32-bit Compiler Topic and Calling Convention subtopic.

You must be careful when changing the default calling convention. For example, the following sample will produce an Undefined symbol _main . . . if you specify the Pascal-style as the default calling convention.

```
#include <stdio.h>


void ShowMessage( char *msg )
{
    printf( msg );
}

int main( void )
{
    ShowMessage ( "Hello! \n" );
    return 0;
}
```

The error is a result of the Pascal naming convention that assigns the function main( ) the internal name MAIN. The compiler's library, on the other hand, is looking for a function named _main, expecting the default C naming convention. To eliminate the error message, you must use the __cdecl keyword when defining main.

```
int __cdecl main( void )
{
    /* ... */
    return 0;
}
```

__fastcall

Parameters are commonly passed on the stack. You can, however, write a function that expects its parameters in registers by using the __fastcall function modifier. There are restrictions regarding the number and type of parameters that can be passed with registers. As a general rule, use the __fastcall convention only with functions expecting no more than three parameters of the type char, int, unsigned, long, or near pointers.

```
/* ************************************************** */
/* FASTCALL.C: Function using __fastcall convention. */
/* ************************************************** */


#include <stdio.h>
#include <conio.h>


int __fastcall Sum( int a, int b, int c )
{
```

```
        return a+b+c+d;
}


int main( void )
{
        int x=10, y=20, z=30;
        printf( "The sum is %d\n", Sum( x, y, z ) );
        return 0;
}
```

The internal name of a function using the **__fastcall** calling convention is the name defined by the programmer prefixed with an at-sign (@). The internal name of our function Sum, therefore, is *@Sum*.

You can specify the __fastcall convention as the default by

- using the -pr compiler command line option

or

- selecting Register from the Project_Options dialog, 16-bit Compiler, or 32-bit Compiler Topic and Calling Convention subtopic.

__stdcall

The standard calling convention, specified by the **__stdcall** modifier, can be used only when building a 32-bit application.

```
void __stdcall SaveThreadData( void *p )
{
        /* ... */
}
```

It is a hybrid of the C and Pascal style. Parameters are pushed on the stack from right to left. The callee is responsible, however, for cleaning the stack. There is no difference between the name of a function using the __stdcall modifier and its internal name assigned by the compiler. The internal name of the function SaveThreadData is *SaveThreadData*.

You can make the __stdcall convention the default by

- using the -ps compiler command line option

or

- selecting Standard Call from the Project_Options dialog, 32-bit Compiler Topic, and Calling Convention subtopic.

Inline Assembly

Nothing compares to assembly language when efficiency and direct control is required. Assembly language code, however, is usually not portable and, for most of us, demands attention to tedious details. As a compromise, you can use the __**asm** keyword to embed assembly language statements in your C function. You may even have the assembly section interact with your C functions and variables. If you want to use more than one assembly language statement, enclose them within braces.

```
/* ************************************************** */
/* BASM1.C: Example using inline assembly...        */
/* ************************************************** */

#include <stdio.h>

int num1 = 125;
int num2 = 300;
```

```
int main( void )
{
  printf( "num1=%d,  num2=%d \n", num1, num2 );

  /* Quick assembly routine to load two     */
  /* numbers in registers                    */
  /* and swap them using xors...             */
  asm {
          mov    ax,    num1
          mov    dx,    num2
          xor    ax,    dx
          xor    dx,    ax
          xor    ax,    dx
          mov    num1, ax;    mov    num2, dx
      }

  printf( "num1=%d,  num2=%d \n", num1, num2 );
  return 0;
}
```

You can create labels within the __**asm** block and use them as targets for branching. You can also call other C functions from the __**asm** block.

```
/* ********************************************** */
/* BASM2.C: Example using inline assembly...      */
/* ********************************************** */

#include <stdio.h>

void __near ShowMsg()
{
    printf( "Hello from nearby!\n" );
}
```

```c
void __far ShowMsgF()
{
    printf( "Hello from far away!\n" );
}


int main( void )
{
    asm {
            mov   cx, 3
      LBL01:
            call near ptr ShowMsg
            call far  ptr ShowMsgF
            loop LBL01
        }
    return 0;
}
```

When calling functions that take parameters, make sure that you push
the arguments on the stack before executing the call instruction. You
may also need to clean up the stack after the call instruction. If you are
likely to recompile code using the call statement under different memory
models, you may consider using the preprocessor to conditionally use a
near or far call.

```c
/* ************************************************ */
/* BASM3.C: Example using inline assembly...        */
/* ************************************************ */

#include <stdio.h>

#define  COUNT  55


void ShowCount( int cnt )
{
```

```
        printf( "The count is %d!\n", cnt );
}


int main( void )
{
    asm {
            mov    ax, COUNT      /* Push parameter   */
            push   ax            /* on stack...       */
#if defined(__TINY__) ¦¦ defined(__SMALL__) \
                  ¦¦ defined(__MEDIUM__)
            call   near ptr ShowCount
#else
            call   far  ptr ShowCount
#endif
            pop    cx            /* Clean up stack.. */
        }
    return 0;
}
```

Pseudo Registers

Borland C++ provides the following keywords for direct manipulation of
the CPU registers and flags:

_AX	_AL	_AH	_SI	_ES
_BX	_BL	_BH	_DI	_SS
_CX	_CL	_CH	_BP	_CS
_DX	_DL	_DH	_SP	_DS
_FLAGS				

These keywords can be treated as global variables and used as such. If you enable the 386 instruction set while compiling, you also may use these additional keywords that map to the 386-specific registers:

_EAX	_EBX	_ECX	_EDX
_ESI	_EDI	_ESP	_EBP

Beware of Side-Effects when Using Pseudo Registers

You must be very careful when using pseudo registers as some statements may result in side-effects destroying the contents of other registers. For instance, this sample

```c
#include <dos.h>

char msg[] = "Hello!";

void f()
{
    _AH = 0x09;
    _DX = FP_OFF( msg );
    _DS = FP_SEG( msg );
    geninterrupt( 0x21 );
}
```

will not work as expected because the assignment of the DS register will result in the temporary use of the AX register, destroying the value of AH. For this reason, it's often best to use inline assembly instead of pseudo registers.

Summary

The extensions in this chapter are best restricted to a few routines or modules in a project so that the code can be recompiled easily across the environments supported by Borland C++ (DOS, Windows 16-bit, and Windows 32-bit) and so that a port to non-INTEL platforms remains simple. The gain in performance achievable with (inline) assembly language or the luxury of (huge) pointer normalization offers flexible opportunities to any program targeting the personal computer.

Chapter 5
Moving to C++

C++ is based on C. This means that your C programs can easily be recompiled as C++ programs. There are, however, a few constructs that C and C++ treat differently, so you may need to make a few modifications to your existing C code. On the other hand, C++ provides various enhancements for the C programmer. Several of the extensions provided by C++ do not require the use of objects and can be readily incorporated in your C code. This chapter is divided in three sections. The first part looks at the cases where C and C++ differ in interpretation. If you have several lines of C code and have been thinking of taking advantage of

C++, this section will provide a checklist of items that you need to look for in your code. In the second part, you will learn about several C++ features which, hopefully, will make the migration from C to C++ look attractive and enticing. The last section will provide information on how to interface C++ with non-C++ code. This is particularly important if you are using non-C++ libraries or work on a project with other programmers using C, Assembly, or Pascal.

How C++ Differs from ANSI C

The best method to port C programs to C++ is to just recompile the code as C++ and address all warnings and possible errors as you move along. This allows the compiler to spot the invalid constructs or suspicious idioms. The following section covers the conflicts you will probably encounter and offers solutions to smooth the transition.

C++ Keywords

C++ adds to the list of keywords reserved by C. When converting existing C code to C++, you must check that none of the C++ keywords are used as identifiers in your C code. The following is a list of the C++ keywords to watch for:

asm

catch

class

delete

friend

inline

new

operator

private

protected

public

template

this

throw

try

virtual

Function Prototypes

ANSI C supports function prototyping but does not require it. Borland C++ will usually issue a warning when a function is called without a prototype within a C program. C++, on the other hand, will issue an error: `You must declare a function before using it!`

void*

C allows a void* to be assigned to a variable of any pointer type. In C++, you need an explicit cast for such conversions. The following code is fine in C but generates a `cannot cast 'void*' to 'char*'` error message when recompiled as C++.

```
#include  <stdlib.h>

char *p = NULL;

void AllocateMemory()
{
     p = malloc( sizeof( char ) * 1024 );
}
```

Changing the assignment to include an explicit cast eliminates the error message when using C++:

```
p = ( char* )malloc( sizeof( char ) * 1024 );
```

Global const Variables and Linkage

A global const variable has external linkage by default in C. In C++, you must precede the keyword const with the extern keyword if global linkage is necessary.

Using C++ Headers with const in C

It is interesting to note that this difference may also result in duplicate symbol error messages at link time if a C++ header file that contains const variables is used by more than one C file in a project.

Character Constant Type

The type of a character constant is char in C++. C uses an int for that purpose. This is unlikely to cause an error. However, you must verify that your code does not assume that sizeof(c) equals sizeof(int).

Skipping Initialization

C allows some constructs that may skip the initialization of a variable; C++ does not. For example, the following C code generates a Case bypasses initialization of a local variable when compiled as C++.

```c
#include <windows.h>


LRESULT CALLBACK _export WndProc( HWND hwnd, UINT msg,
                                  WPARAM wParam, LPARAM lParam )
{
    switch( msg )
    {
        unsigned key = 0;

        case WM_LBUTTONDOWN:
            key = ( unsigned )wParam;
            if ( key & MK_SHIFT )
            {
              /* ... */
            }

        case WM_MOUSEMOVE:
            break;
    }
    return 0;
}
```

To eliminate the error message, you can declare the variable *key* within a block after the WM_LBUTTONDOWN: case.

C++ as an Improved C

This section takes a look at the C++ features that make C++ a better C.

Default Arguments

When prototyping a function in C++, you can specify default values for some of the parameters. This allows you to leave out the corresponding arguments when calling the function, and the compiler will use the default values. Default parameters must be consecutive. If you assign a default value to a parameter, you must also assign default values to any parameters to the right. Similarly, when you call the function, if you omit a default parameter, you must omit all parameters to the right. Specify the default arguments only in the function prototype, not in the function definition. Look at some examples:

```
//
// Prototypes function 'ShowMessage' with two
// default parameters
//
void ShowMessage( char *msg, int x=0, int y=0 );


//
// The following is incorrect: all parameters to the right
// of a parameter with default value must all be assigned
// default values.
```

```
//
void ShowMsg( int x=0, int y=0, char *msg );


//
//This call to ShowMessage is incorrect; choosing the
//default value for the second parameter requires that
//the default value of the third parameter be used
//
ShowMessage( "Error: Out of Memory", ,10 );


//
//These calls to ShowMessage are correct
//
ShowMessage( "Error: Out of Memory" );
ShowMessage( "Error: Out of Memory, 10, 10 );
ShowMessage( "Error: Out of Memory, 10 );
```

Default Values: Not Just Constants!

The default value of a function argument is not limited to constants;
it can be a global variable or even the value returned by a function.

```
////////////////////////////////////////////////////////////
// DEFARG.CPP  Sample with default function arguments//
////////////////////////////////////////////////////////////

#include <stdio.h>
#include <stdlib.h>
#include <errno.h>
```

```
/////////////////////////////////////////////////
// Use Global variable errno as default value..
void ShowError( int errValue = errno );


/////////////////////////////////////////////////
void ShowError( int errValue )
{
    printf( "ERROR: %s \n", sys_errlist[errValue] );
}


/////////////////////////////////////////////////
int main( void )
{
    fopen( "\\DOES\\NOT\\EXIST.TXT", "r" );
    ShowError();           // Use Default argument, errno!

    ShowError( ENOMEM );// Not enough memory error

    return 0;
}
```

Reference

C++ offers a slight variation to pointers in the form of *references*. A reference can be viewed as a pointer to a particular variable which is always dereferenced when used. However, a reference does not occupy additional memory space: it is merely another name or alias for the variable. The unary **&** operator is used to declare a reference. The following illustrates:

```
//////////////////////////////////////////////////////////
// REF.CPP: Using C++ references...                      //
//////////////////////////////////////////////////////////

#include <stdio.h>

int  value  = 10;
int &refval = value;      // Reference to value

int main( void )
{
    printf( "value = %d \n", value );

    refval += 5;            // Modifies value via refval
    printf( "value = %d \n", value );

    printf( "address of value  is %p \n", &value  );
    printf( "address of refval is %p \n", &refval );

    return 0;
}
```

References are primarily used for function parameters and for function return types. A reference, however, also can be declared to as an alias for another variable as shown in the preceding example. In this case, the reference must be initialized when declared unless it is declared as *extern*. A reference cannot be assigned another variable after initialization.

Reference Parameters

C passes parameters by value. This means that the compiler makes a copy of the variables specified by the caller for the callee. When the callee needs to modify the caller's variable, a pointer to the latter is passed. The callee then can dereference the pointer to modify the caller's copy of the variable. C++ references let you pass arguments by reference. Calling a function expecting a *reference variable* follows the same syntax used when passing variables by value. However, in the case of references, the callee can modify the caller's copy of the variable. You can indicate that a function expects a reference parameter by preceding the variable with the **&** modifier when prototyping the function. The following example illustrates the use of reference parameters.

```
////////////////////////////////////////////////////////
// REF_PARM.CPP: Sample using reference variable...  //
////////////////////////////////////////////////////////

#include <stdio.h>


void Inc_val( int  i )  // Receives parameter by value
{
    i++;                // Increment does not affect original
}


void Inc_ptr( int *i )  // Receives address of caller's copy
{
    (*i)++;             // Modifies caller's copy via
}                       // indirection


void Inc_ref( int &i )  // Receives a reference
{
    i++;                // Modifies caller's copy!!
}
```

```c
int main( void )
{
    int j=10;
    printf( "J is %d\n", j );

    Inc_val( j );
    printf( "After Inc_val(j),  j=%d\n", j );

    Inc_ptr( &j );
    printf( "After Inc_ptr(&j), j=%d\n", j );

    Inc_ref( j );
    printf( "After Inc_ref(j),  j=%d\n", j );

    return 0;
}
```

When you call a function expecting a reference, the compiler indirectly passes the address of the parameter you specified to the function. Within the function itself, the compiler translates all references to the parameter by dereferencing the address passed. This is all done behind the scenes! The main advantage of references over pointers is in the simplicity of the code:

- The caller does not need the address of operator (&).

- The callee avoids the clumsy indirection operators (*, ->).

References are also very useful when passing large structures because passing an address is more efficient than copying a whole structure.

Function with Reference Return Type

References can be used for the return type of a function. This allows the function to be assigned a value. For example, consider the following:

```
/////////////////////////////////////////////////////
//  REF_RET.CPP: Reference for function return type..  //
/////////////////////////////////////////////////////

#include  <stdio.h>

const    int  arraySize = 0xF;
static  int  valArray[arraySize];

int&  valueAt( int  indx )
{
      return  valArray[indx];
}

int  main( void )
{
```

```
    for( int i=0; i<arraySize; i++ )
        valueAt( i ) = 1 << i;

    for( i=0; i<arraySize; i++ )
        printf( "value at %02d = %-6d\n", i, valueAt( i ) );

    return 0;
}
```

The function *valueAt(int)* can be used to read the value at a particular index and assign a new value to that location.

Data Abstraction via Reference Return Type

You can use a function that returns a reference to a variable to *hide* the variable and to monitor its accesses. For example, the *valueAt* function could be rewritten as the following:

```
#include <assert.h>

int& valueAt( int indx )
{
    assert( indx >= 0 );
    assert( indx < arraySize );
    return valArray[indx];
}
```

By making the array (*valArray*) static and restricting all interaction with the variable to the function *valueAt()*, the code ensures that all accesses are within the bounds of the array. The use of such techniques can help reduce errors in projects.

Inline Functions

The *inline* keyword is a function modifier. It instructs the compiler to expand the function's body in place whenever it is called instead of executing a function call. Function inlining generally speeds up your code because the overhead of a function call is avoided. However, inlining large functions may increase the size of your application. It is customary to inline small functions such as the swap routine in the following example.

```
///////////////////////////////////////////////////
// INLINE.CPP: Sample code with inline function...   //
///////////////////////////////////////////////////

#include <stdio.h>

inline void swap( int &i, int &j )
{
    i ^= j ^= i ^= j;
}


int main( void )
{
    int a = 10, b = 20;

    printf( "a= %d  -  b = %d \n", a, b );
    swap( a, b );
    printf( "a= %d  -  b = %d \n", a, b );
    return 0;
}
```

Restrictions on Inline Functions

Borland C++ will not inline the following:

- Functions containing while, do/while, switch/case, for, and goto statements

- Non-void functions without a return statement

- Functions with inline assembly

Inline Function Definition

The definition of an inline function must precede any call to the function. For this reason, it is a good idea to put inline functions in a header file. In the following example, the function min() is called before its definition. The compiler generates the error Function defined inline after use as extern.

```
int i, j;

int min( int i1, int i2 );

int main( void )
{
    return min( i, j );
}

inline int min( int i1, int i2 )
{
    return i1 > i2 ? i2 : i1;
}
```

The error message can be eliminated if the keyword inline is included in the function prototype. However, if the function is called before its definition, the compiler generates a call instead of expanding the function inline. The following example illustrates:

```
int i, j, k, l;

inline int max( int i1, int i2 );

int func1( void )
{
    return max( i, j ); // Not expanded inline !!
}

inline int max( int i1, int i2 )
{
    return i1 > i2 ? i2 : i1;
}

int func2( void )
{
    return max( k, l ); // Expanded inline !!
}
```

The :: Operator

In C, a local variable hides any global variable with the same name. All references to the name within the scope of the local variable refer to the local variable. C++ allows you to access the global variable by prefixing the variable name with ::, the **scope resolution operator**. The following example demonstrates the use of the scope resolution operator. Note that the operator allows access to global variables even if there is a variable with a similar name in an outer local scope.

```
///////////////////////////////////////////////////////
// SCOPE.CPP:  Illustrates the scope resolution oper.//
///////////////////////////////////////////////////////
```

```
#include <stdio.h>

int total = 10;                    // Global variable

int main( void )
{                                  //
    int total = 100;               // Local variable in
                                   // outer scope
                                   //

    if ( total > 0 )
    {                              //
        int total = 1000;          // Local in inner scope
                                   //

        printf( "local  total : %d \n",   total );
        printf( "global total : %d \n", ::total );
    }
    return 0;
}
```

Overloaded Functions

In C, every function must have a unique name. C++ allows you to declare
functions with similar names but unique argument types. This feature
contributes to readability because a single *overloaded* name describes
one common process which may be performed on various data types.
The compiler uses the appropriate function by matching the argument
types. The following example overloads the function *ShowMessage* to
accept either a string or integer:

```
///////////////////////////////////////////////////
// OVERLOAD.CPP: Using Overloaded functions...      //
///////////////////////////////////////////////////
```

```
#include <stdlib.h>
#include <stdio.h>

void ShowMessage( int );
void ShowMessage( char *msg );


void ShowMessage( int errCode )
{
    printf( "MSG: %s \n", sys_errlist[errCode] );
}


void ShowMessage( char *msg )
{
    printf( "MSG: %s \n", msg );
}

int main( void )
{
    ShowMessage( 1 );    // 1: Invalid function number!!
    ShowMessage( "Error corrected!" );
    return 0;
}
```

Restrictions

- Functions differing only in their return types cannot be overloaded. For example, the following generates a Type mismatch in redeclaration error message because the compiler considers only the arguments:

int getCustInfo(char *name); // returns Accnt number

char *getCustInfo(char *name); // returns cust. address

- Functions cannot be overloaded if their parameter(s) only differs by the use of the *const* or *volatile* modifiers, or by a reference. The errors generated for the following example illustrate:

void DelRec(int indx);

void DelRec(int &indx);

void DelRec(const int indx);

void DelRec(volatile int indx);

'DelRec(int &)' cannot be distinguished from 'DelRec(int)'

'DelRec(const int)' cannot be distinguished from 'DelRec(int)'

'DelRec(volatile int)' cannot be distinguished from 'DelRec(int)'

Implementation: Name Mangling

At the basis of function overloading is a feature of C++ commonly referred to as *name mangling* or *name decoration*. The compiler internally appends some characters to a function name indicating the type and order of parameters expected by the function. For example, the following table lists the internal names of some overloaded functions.

void func(int i);	@func$qi
int func(int i);	@func$qi
void func(char c);	@func$qc
void func(char *p);	@func$qpc

Note how the internal names of the first two functions are identical, although they differ in their return type. The appendix of this book contains a table with a list and description of the various sequences used by Borland C++ when mangling names.

Variable Declaration

In C, local variables must be declared at the beginning of a block. This implies that local declarations must precede program statements. C++ allows you to declare a variable anywhere. This reduces the possibility of errors because variables are declared closer to the code that uses them. See the following example:

```
////////////////////////////////////////////////////
// LOCALVAR.CPP: Flexible variable declaration...    //
////////////////////////////////////////////////////

#include <stdio.h>

int main( void )
{
    printf( Hello there! \n );

    int i;
    printf( The value of i = %d \n, i );

    for( int j=0; j<10; j++ )
    {
        printf( j=%d , j );
    }

    printf( \nThe current value of j = %d, j );

    return 0;
}
```

The preceding example uses a common C++ construct where the counter of a *for* loop is declared and initialized within the for statement. Notice that the counter, *j*, is still accessible outside of the *for* block.

Const Values

In C, the *const* modifier implies that a variable may not be modified after being initialized. C++, on the other hand, treats *const* variables as true constant expressions. So, unlike C, C++ allows the use of *const* variable to specify the size of an array.

```
///////////////////////////////////////////////////////
// CNSTARRY.CPP: Using const variable for array size //
///////////////////////////////////////////////////////

const  unsigned numSqr = 8*8;
unsigned board[numSqr];
```

Enum, struct, and union Tags

In C++ an enum tag name, struct tag name, or union tag name is a type name. Therefore, the keyword *struct*, *union*, or *enum* is not necessary when declaring a variable. For example:

```
enum Account { edu, corp, persnl };

struct custInfo
{
    char    name[80];
    long    acctNum;
    Account AccType;    // instead of 'enum Account accType'
};

custInfo c = { "FD, Ltd.", 100, corp }; // no struct keyword!!
```

Anonymous Unions

C++ supports a special type of union referred to as *anonymous unions*. These unions have no tag name. The union members share the same area of memory and can be accessed by name. Global anonymous unions must be declared static. The following example illustrates both global and local anonymous unions:

```
/////////////////////////////////////////////////////
// ANOUNION.CPP: Illustrates anonymous unions...    //
/////////////////////////////////////////////////////

#include <string.h>

//
// custName and custID share the same area in memory
//
static union {
            char custName[80];
            long custID;
          };

int main( void )
{
   //
   // A local anonymous union - newID and counter share
   // the same area of memory
   //
   union {
          int newID;
          int counter;
        };

   for( counter=0; counter<10; counter++ )
      custID = counter;
```

```
    strcpy( custName, "NEW" );
    newID = 0x100;


    return 0;
}
```

Flexible Memory Allocation Operators

C++ provides the *new* and *delete* (and *new[]* and *delete[]*) operators for handling dynamic memory allocation. Traditionally, C programs use the *malloc*, *calloc*, and *free* library routines instead. Like all C functions, these can still be called from C++. However, the C++ operators offer enhancements:

- new returns a pointer of the type memory is being allocated for, and malloc returns a void pointer. A cast, therefore, is not required when using new. The following is an example:

```
#include <stdlib.h>
#include <stdio.h>

long *lptr;

void f1( void )
{
    lptr = ( long* )malloc( sizeof( long ) );
   *lptr = 0x1000;
    printf( "The value is %ld \n", *lptr );
    free( lptr );
}

void f2( void )
{
```

```
    lptr = new long;
   *lptr = 1000;
    printf( "The value is %ld \n", *lptr );
    delete lptr;
    return 0;
}
```

- Along with the new operator, C++ provides a library function, *set_new_handler()*, which you can use to install a user-defined error handler. The handler is called whenever a memory allocation error occurs. The following example illustrates a user-defined new handler:

```
/////////////////////////////////////////////////////////
// NEWHNDLR.CPP: Using a user-defined new handler... //
/////////////////////////////////////////////////////////

#include <stdio.h>
#include <stdlib.h>
#include <new.h>

void MyNewHandler()
{
    printf( "Out of memory! \n" );
    exit(1);
}

int main( void )
{
    // Install new handler
    set_new_handler( MyNewHandler );

    // ...  More code goes here ... //

    return 0;
}
```

- The flexibility of the new and delete operators are most evident when using classes because a class can define its own version of the new and delete operators. The new and delete operators also invoke special initialization and cleanup routines for classes, if present. The global version of the new and delete operators, however, can be overridden for non-class objects and for objects without new and delete operators. This technique is often used by C++ libraries for debugging purposes. Look at the four relevant operators:

```
void* operator new( size_t );

void* operator new[] ( size_t );
```

The new operator is used for all allocations except when you allocate an array. The new[] operator is used when allocating arrays.

```
void operator delete( void* );

void operator delete[] ( void* );
```

Similarly, the delete operator is used for all calls to delete except when deleting an array. The delete[] operator is used when deleting an array.

The new operator also can be overloaded to accept additional parameters. The following example illustrates overridden global new and global delete operators. An overloaded version of new accepting two additional parameters is also included.

```
//////////////////////////////////////////////////
// NEWDEL.CPP: Redefining operator new and delete..  //
//////////////////////////////////////////////////
#include <stdio.h>
#include <stdlib.h>

//
// Override global new operator
//
void* operator new( size_t size )
{
    printf( "new() requested %u bytes \n", size );
    return malloc( size );
}


//
// Override global delete operator
//
void operator delete( void *p )
{
    printf( "delete() \n" );
    free( p );
}


//
// Override global new[] operator
//
void* operator new[]( size_t size )
{
```

```
        printf( "new[] () requested %u bytes \n", size );
        return malloc( size );
}


//
// Override global delete[] operator
//
void operator delete[]( void *p )
{
        printf( "delete[] () \n" );
        free( p );
}


//
// Overload globa new operator...
//
void* operator new( size_t size, char *fname, int line )
{
        printf( "new() from %s at line %d \n", fname, line );
        return malloc( size );
}


int main( void )
{
        int *p = new int;       // calls global new operator
        *p      = 10;
        delete p;               // calls global delete operator

        p       = new int[10]; // calls global new[]
        for( int i=0; i<10; i++ )
            p[i] = i*10;
        delete [] p;            // calls global delete[]
```

```
                          // calls overloaded global new
p        = new (__FILE__, __LINE__) int;
*p       = 10;
delete p;                 // call global delete operator

return 0;
}
```

Overloading new To Track Memory Allocations

The preceding technique can be used to track memory allocations and deletions. By overloading *new* and *delete*, you can add routines to catch double deletions, memory overwrites, leaks, and so on.

new Operator and Placement Syntax

You may overload the new operator so that memory is allocated from a specific address. The syntax is referred to as the *placement syntax* as shown:

```
/////////////////////////////////////////////////////////
// PLACENEW: Using new placement syntax...             //
/////////////////////////////////////////////////////////
```

```
#include <new.h>

int __i = 0;



//
// new operator allowing placement syntax
//
void * operator new ( size_t, void *p )
{
    return p;
}

int main( void )
{
    // Allocate integer as address of __i;
    int *pi = new (&__i) int;

    *pi = 20;

    return 0;
}
```

Note: The *placement syntax* is commonly used to 'call' a constructor for an existing object. See chapter 6 for more information.

Interfacing C++ to C, Assembly, and Pascal

A project may require the use of C++ code with a C, Assembly, or Pascal Library. You also may have to write some C++ functions that are called from non C++ code. To accommodate these scenarios, *name mangling* must be disabled. C++ provides *linkage specifications* for that purpose.

Linkage Specification

Linkage specification can be used for two purposes:

- Instruct the compiler not to name mangle a C++ function you are defining.

- Inform the compiler that an external function you are calling does not use the C++ linkage.

The following example illustrates both cases:

```
/////////////////////////////////////////////////////////
// TYPELINK.CPP: Linkage specification...              //
/////////////////////////////////////////////////////////
#include <stdio.h>


extern "C"  void CppFuncCalledFromC( void );



extern "C" {
        void FunctionInCLibrary( void );
        void FunctionInASMLibrary( int );
        }
```

```
void CppFuncCalledFromC( void )
{
    printf( "Hello !\n" );
}

void func( int i )
{
    FunctionInCLibrary();
    FunctionInASMLibrary( i );
}
```

The Borland C++ compiler supports two languages for linkage specification: C and C++.

Linkage Specification and Calling Convention

It is important to differentiate a function's calling convention from its linkage specification. For example, Windows programs often require several callback functions that use the PASCAL calling convention. If you don't want the compiler to mangle these function names, use the C linkage specification as shown in the following example:

```
//////////////////////////////////////////////////////////
// PASCAL.CPP: Calling convention vs. Link Spec...    //
//////////////////////////////////////////////////////////
#include <windows.h>

// InitCallback must not be mangled!
extern "C" BOOL FAR PASCAL _export InitCallback( UINT );
```

```
// InfoCallback is mangled!
BOOL FAR PASCAL _export InfoCallback( UINT );
```

In the above example, the internal names generated by the compiler for the two callback functions—InitCallback and InfoCallback—are INITCALLBACK and @INFOCALLBACK$QUI respectively.

Header Files

If you are using C++ but need to call functions written in C, you can include the C-language headers within a C linkage-specification block as shown:

```
//////////////////////////////////////////////////////
// CPP_N_C.CPP: Using C Libraries...                 //
//////////////////////////////////////////////////////

extern "C"
{
#include "clibfunc.h"
#include "asmfunc.h"
}
```

If you are writing C++ functions that will be called from non-C++ code, you can provide a header file that uses the C linkage-specification when compiling in C++ mode. The following is a sample header:

```
#if defined(__cplusplus)   // Check if we're in C++ mode
extern "C"  {              // If yes, use "C" link spec.
#endif                     // (__cplusplus)
```

```
// Here goes the function prototypes


#if defined(__cplusplus)   // C++ mode ?
     }                      // End C Linkage block
#endif                      // (_ _cplusplus)
```

The preceding header relies on the _ _*cplusplus* macro defined by the
compiler when in C++ mode.

Summary

You've now seen miscellaneous C++ enhancements that can be readily
used in existing C code. The next chapter will look at the foundation of
Object Oriented Programming in the C++ Language: C++ classes!

Chapter 6

Object-Oriented Programming in C++

This chapter explores the object-oriented aspect of C++. You will see the language's features that allow you to create data types, produce reusable code, and better control your program's structure. The terms associated with object-oriented programming, such as *polymorphism* or *inheritance* are also examined. Although the object-oriented features of C++ are different from the procedural aspects of C, you should be familiar with the basics of the C language before going through this chapter.

C++ Class

A class is the fundamental mechanism by which C++ introduces object oriented features to the C language. A class is an extension of the C struct. It allows you to create types and to define functions that dictate the behavior of the type. Each instance of a class is called an *object*. In a way, you can view a class as a means to extend the language.

Defining a Class

A *class* definition is similar to that of a C structure definition except that:

- It usually contains one or more *access specifiers* denoted by the keywords *public*, *protected*, or *private*.

- The *class* or *union* keyword may be used in place of *struct*.

- It usually contains functions (*member functions* or *methods*) as well as data members.

- It usually contains some special functions such as a function with the same name as the class itself (*constructor*) or a function with the class's name and a tilde (~) as a prefix (*destructor*).

The following sample illustrates a few class definitions:

```
/////////////////////////////////////////////////////
// CLASSDEF.CPP: Sample class definitions...        //
/////////////////////////////////////////////////////

//
// class Rect ( similar to C-structs )
//
struct Rect
{
```

```
    int x1;      //
    int y1;      // Rect's Data
    int x2;      // Members...
    int y2;      //
};



//
// class Point: contains both data members
//              and member functions...
//              Also uses access specifiers
//
struct Point
{
    private:     // 'private' access specifier
        int x;   // Data members of class
        int y;   // type 'Point'


    public:      // 'public' access specifier
        int  GetX();     //
        int  GetY();     // Member functions of
        void SetX(int);  // class type 'Point'
        void SetY(int);  //
};



//
// class Line
//
class Line
{
    Point pt1;     //
    Point pt2;     // Data members...
    int width;     //
```

```
    public:                     // 'public' access specifier
        Line(int _x, int _y); // Member function: Constructor!
        ~Line();                // Member function: Destructor!
};
```

In the preceding example, the definition of the class *Rect* is similar to that of a C structure definition. The class *Point* contains *access specifiers* and member functions. Unlike *Rect* or *Point*, the class *Line* was defined with the *class* keyword, and it contains some special member functions. The following sections examine access specifiers, the three class keywords, and member functions.

Access Control

In C, the members of a structure are freely accessible to any functions within the scope of the structure. This often leads to inadvertent modifications of data. With C++, you can restrict the visibility of class data members and member functions with the use of the *public, protected,* or *private* labels. An access specifier label applies to all the members following the label until another label is encountered or until the class definition ends. The following table describes the three access specifiers:

Table 6.1 Class Access Specifiers

Access Label	Description
private:	Data members and member functions are only accessible to member functions of the same class.

Access Label	Description
public:	Data members and member functions can be accessed by member functions and other functions of the program with an instance of the class.
protected:	Data members and member functions can be accessed by the member functions of the same class and by the member functions of classes derived from this class.

Classes, Structures, and Unions

In C++ a *struct*, a *class*, and a *union* are considered class types. A *struct* and a *class* are alike except for their default access specifiers: a *struct* defaults to *public;* whereas a class defaults to *private*. Like a *struct*, a *union* defaults to public. Like the C *unions*, the data members of a C++ *union* start at the same memory location.

The following table summarizes the differences among the three types:

Table 6.2 Difference among class, struct, and union

	Classes	Structs	Unions
Keyword:	class	struct	union
Default Access:	private	public	public
Data Overlaps:	No	No	Yes

Class Members

The members of a class fall into two main groups:

- data, referred to as data members
- code, referred to as member functions or methods

Data Members

Data members of C++ classes are similar to the members of C structures with a few enhancements. The following list outlines the attributes of class data members:

- Data members cannot be declared as *auto*, *extern*, or *register*.
- Data members can be enums, bit-fields, or instances of previously declared classes.
- A data member of a class cannot be an instance of the class itself.
- A data member of a class can be a pointer or reference to an instance of the class.

Member Functions

A *member function* is a function *declared* within the definition of a class. The body of the function may also be *defined* within the class definition; the *member function* then is referred to as an *inline* member function. When the body of a member function is defined outside the body of a class, the function's name is prefixed with the class name and the scoping operator (::). The function is then referred to as an *out_of_line* member function. The following example illustrates both inline and out-of-line member functions:

```cpp
//////////////////////////////////////////////////////////
// MEMFUNC.CPP Class with member functions...        //
//////////////////////////////////////////////////////////
#include <assert.h>

const int MAX_X = 0x100;
const int MAX_Y = 0x100;

struct Point
{
    private:
        int x;
        int y;

    public:
        int  GetX()
        {
            return x;
        }

        int  GetY()
        {
            return y;
        }

        void SetX(int);
        void SetY(int);
};
```

```
void Point::SetX(int _x)
{
    assert( _x >= 0 );
    assert( _x <= MAX_X );
    x = _x;
}


void Point::SetY(int _y)
{
    assert( _y >= 0 );
    assert( _y <= MAX_Y);
    y = _y;
}
```

The method functions *GetX* and *GetY* are both inline, but *SetX* and *SetY* are out-of-line. You can define an inline member function outside of the body of the class by preceding the function definition header with the *inline* keyword. The following example illustrates:

```
////////////////////////////////////////////////////////
// INLINEF.CPP: Inline Member Functions...           //
////////////////////////////////////////////////////////

class Time
{
        int hr, min;

    public:
        void SetTime(int, int);
        void GetTime(int&, int&);
};

inline void Time::SetTime(int _hr, int _min)
{
    hr  = _hr;
```

```
    min = _min;
}

inline void Time::GetTime(int &hour, int &minute)
{
    hour   = hr;
    minute = min;
}
```

Class Scope

C supports four kinds of scope: function, file, block, and function proto-type (see Chapter 2). C++ introduces the concept of *class scope*: the names of all the members of a class are within the scope of the class—they can be used by the member functions of the class. The members of a class can also be used in the following cases:

- With instances of the class (or classes derived from it) followed by the . operator

  [instance.member_name].

- With instances of pointers to the class (or classes derived from it) followed by the **->** operator

  [instanceptr->member_name].

- With the class name followed by the **::** scope resolution operator

  [classname::member_name].

Accessing Data Members

Member functions are in the scope of the class in which they are defined. They can, therefore, access any data member of the class by using the name of the variable. Regular functions or member functions of other classes can access the data members using the . or -> operators with instances or pointers to instances of the class respectively. The following example illustrates:

```cpp
///////////////////////////////////////////////////////
// DATAMEM.CPP: Accessing Class Data Members...        //
///////////////////////////////////////////////////////

class Coord
{
    public:
        int x, y;
};


int main( void )
{
    Coord  org;              // Create local object
    Coord *orgPtr = &org;    // Create pointer to local object

    org.x     = 0;           // Using object.member
    orgPtr->y = 0;           // Using objectPtr->member

    return 0;
}
```

Calling Member Functions

Member functions of a class can call other member functions of the class by using the name of the function. Regular functions or member functions of other classes can call the member functions by using the . or -> operators with an instance of the class or pointer to an instance of the class respectively. The following example illustrates:

```cpp
/////////////////////////////////////////////////////////
// CODEMEM.CPP: Accessing Class Member Functions...  //
/////////////////////////////////////////////////////////

class Coord
{
        int x, y;
    public:
        void SetCoord( int _x, int _y )
        {    x=_x;    y=_y;    }

        void GetCoord( int &_x, int &_y)
        {    _x=x;    _y=y;    }
};


int main( void )
{
    Coord   org;            // Create local object
    Coord *orgPtr = &org;   // Create pointer to local object

    org.SetCoord(10, 10);   // Using object.memberFunc()

    int col, row;
    orgPtr->GetCoord(col, row); // Using objectPtr->member

    return 0;
}
```

Using Pointers to Member Functions

You can declare a pointer to a class member function. The syntax is as follows:

return_Type (ClassName::* ptrName)(params, ...);

To use the pointer, you can use either the operator **->*** or the operator **.***. The following example illustrates how to use a pointer to a member function:

```
//////////////////////////////////////////////////////
// MEMPTR.CPP: Using pointers to member functions... //
//////////////////////////////////////////////////////

#include <stdio.h>

//
// Simple class A
//
class A
{
      int i;
   public:
      A( int _i ) : i(_i) {}

      void Func()
      {  printf( "Hello, i = %d \n", i ); }

      //
      // Function which invokes a member function
      // whose address is passed as parameter
      //
      void CallMemberPtr( void (A::*funcPtr)() )
      {
```

```
            (*this.*funcPtr)();
        }
};


//
// Function which invokes a member function for
// a particular object: both the object and the
// member function are passed as parameters...
//
void UseMemFuncPtr( A *aObjectPtr, void(A::*funcPtr)() )
{
    (aObjectPtr->*funcPtr)();
}


//
// main: Exercises the functions defined above...
//
int main( void )
{
    void (A::*funcPtr)() = &A::Func;

    A a1( 1965 );
    UseMemFuncPtr( &a1, funcPtr );

    A a2( 3435 );
    a2.CallMemberPtr( funcPtr );

    return 0;
}
```

The following rules apply to pointers to member functions:

- A pointer to a member function cannot point to a static member function.

- A pointer to a member function cannot be converted to a regular (non-member) function pointer.

The this *Pointer*

Every non-static member function has access to the object for which it was called with the *this* keyword. The type of *this* is *classType**. The following sample illustrates the use of the *this* pointer.

```
/////////////////////////////////////////////////////
// THISPTR.CPP: Using the this pointer...           //
/////////////////////////////////////////////////////
class Simple
{
    public:
        Simple();
        void Greet()
        {
            printf("Hello!\n");
        }
};

Simple::Simple()
{
    Greet();                // Each statement
    this->Greet();          // of this function
    (*this).Greet();        // calls the
}                           // Greet() function
```

Given that member functions have access to all class members by specifying the name, the *this* pointer is mainly used to return a pointer (in other words, return *this*) or as a reference to the implied object (in other words return **this;*).

Special Member Functions

The term *Special Member Functions* refers to some functions of a class that affect the way an instance of the class is created, copied, converted into other objects, and destroyed. These functions are often implicitly called by the compiler. The following list provides a brief description of the functions:

Table 6.3 Description of Special Member Functions

Function	Description
Constructor:	Initializes instances of the class
Copy Constructor:	Initializes a new instance using the values of an already existing instance
Assignment Operator:	Assigns the contents of an instance to another instance

continues

Table 6.3 continued

Function	Description
Destructor:	Performs cleanup for instances of the class
new operator:	Allocates memory for dynamic instances of class
delete operator:	Frees memory of dynamic instances of class
Conversion Functions:	Converts an instance of the class to another type.

Constructor

A *constructor* is a member function with the same name as its class. It is called by the compiler whenever an instance of the class is created. If you do not define any constructors, a *default constructor* (constructor taking no parameters) is generated by the compiler. The following rules apply to constructors:

- A constructor does not have a return type.

- A constructor cannot return values.

- A constructor is not inherited.

- A constructor cannot be declared as *const, volatile, virtual,* or *static.*

Use Exception Handling and Errors

A constructor cannot return a value to indicate an error during object initialization. You can, however, use the C++ *Exception Handling* mechanism to return an error from a constructor. (See Chapter 9 for more information).

Calling the Constructor of an Existing Object

By making use of the *placement syntax*, you can call the constructor of an existing object. The technique is commonly used for global objects that must be initialized after a particular routine has been called. The following example illustrates:

```
///////////////////////////////////////////////////////////
// CALLCTR.CPP: Using placement syntax to call ctr.. //
///////////////////////////////////////////////////////////
#include <new.h>

//
// new operator allowing placement syntax
//
inline void * operator new( size_t, void *p )
{
    return p;
}

//
// Sample class
//
class SomeObject
{
```

continues

continued

```
    public:
        SomeObject();
};

//
// A global instance of class
//
SomeObject gblInst;


int main( void )
{
    CheckSystem();  // Check system setup

    //
    // Now call constructor on existing object
    //
    new (&gblInst) SomeObject;

    return 0;
}
```

Member Initializer List

The data members of a class are usually initialized in the body of the class's constructor. The constructor definition, however, may also contain a *member initialization list*. A *member initialization list* is a list of data members (and *base* classes) that follow the *function declarator* (function signature) and a colon (:) and are separated by commas. Each member receives one or more parameters used for initialization.

The following example illustrates two similar classes with constructors using two techniques to set up data members. The first technique uses the *member initialization list,* and the second assigns the members their values within the constructor body:

```cpp
/////////////////////////////////////////////////////
// MEMINIT.CPP: Member Initialization vs. Assignment //
/////////////////////////////////////////////////////
class XYValue
{
        int x, y;
    public:
        // Uses Member Initialization List
        XYValue( int _x, int _y ) : x(_x), y(_y)
        {
        }
};


class XYData
{
        int x, y;
    public:
        // Using body of constructor for assignment
        XYData( int _x, int _y )
        {
            x = _x;
            y = _y;
        }
};
```

Const, Reference, and Object Data Members

Although the *member initialization list* is optional for most data members, it is the only mechanism to initialize *const* and *reference* data members. If a class data member is an object whose constructor requires one or more parameters, the *member initialization list* is the only mechanism to initialize the object.

Copy Constructor

A *copy constructor* is a special kind of constructor: it takes as its argument a const reference to an object of the class (*const classType&*) or a reference to an object of the class (*classType&*).

```
//////////////////////////////////////////////////////////
// COPYCON.CPP: Class Copy Constructor...              //
//////////////////////////////////////////////////////////

class Coord
{
        int x, y;
    public:
        Coord(const Coord &src);     // Copy constructor
};

Coord::Coord(const Coord &src)       // Copy constructor
{
    x = src.x;
    y = src.y;
}
```

The reference is invoked whenever a new object is initialized with the values of an existing object. A default *copy constructor* is generated by the compiler if you do not provide one. The compiler-generated *copy constructor* performs a literal copy of the object. This is most likely inappropriate for objects containing pointers or references.

Assignment Operator

The *assignment operator* is a member function, with the name *operator=*, which takes a single argument of type *const classType&* (or *classType&*).

The assignment operator is called by the compiler whenever an object is assigned to another object. A default assignment operator is generated by the compiler if you do not provide one. The default operator performs a *bitwise copy*.

```
/////////////////////////////////////////////////////
// ASSGOPER.CPP: Class Assignment operator...       //
/////////////////////////////////////////////////////
```

```
class Coord
{
        int x, y;
    public:
        Coord& operator=(const Coord &src);
};

Coord&  Coord::operator= (const Coord &src)
{
    x = src.x;
    y = src.y;
    return *this;
}
```

Copy Constructor versus Assignment Operator

Although they both copy the data members of an instance of a class to another, you can determine which one will be called by the compiler using the following rule:

- The *assignment operator* is called when the contents of an existing object are changed.

- The *copy constructor* is called when a new object is initialized with the values of another object.

const classType& versus classType&

Both the copy constructor and assignment operator have classType& or const classType& as argument type. The latter is preferred because the former does not allow const objects to be copied.

Declaring a Private Assignment Operator

If your class contains pointers or references, you should probably provide an assignment operator. You also can decide to prevent assignments of the class by declaring the assignment operator in the private section of your class. This will cause the compiler to generate an error message if an assignment is attempted.

Destructor

A *destructor* is the counterpart of the *constructor*. It has the same name as the class preceded with a tilde (~). It is called whenever an instance of the class is destroyed. The following rules applies to destructors:

- A destructor accepts no arguments.
- A destructor cannot return values.
- A destructor is not inherited.
- A destructor cannot be declared as *const, volatile,* or *static.*
- A destructor can be declared as *virtual.*

The compiler generates a default destructor if you do not provide one.

Class's *new* Operator

A class may provide its own versions of the *new* operators:

- The *classType::operator new*, if provided, is called whenever a dynamic object is created.
- The *classType::operator new[]*, if provided, is called whenever a dynamic array of objects is created.

Class's *delete* Operator

A class may provide its own versions of the *delete* operators:

- The *classType::operator delete*, if provided, is called whenever a dynamic object is deleted.

- The *classType::operator delete[]*, if provided, is called whenever a dynamic array of objects is deleted.

The following example illustrates a class with *new* and *delete* operators:

```
//////////////////////////////////////////////////////
// CLASSMEM.CPP: Class providing new/delete operators//
//////////////////////////////////////////////////////

#include <stdio.h>
#include <stdlib.h>
#include <string.h>

//
//  TRACE(msg) macro: displays parameter as string
//
#if !defined(NDEBUG)
#define TRACE(msg) printf( #msg "\n" );
#else
#define TRACE(msg) ((void)0)
#endif

//
// Maximum length of customername
//
const int MAX_NAME = 30;


//
// Sample Data for use as customer names.
//
char *custName[] = {
                    "Maritim Hotel,  Ltd",
                    "Merville Hotel, Ltd",
```

```
                    "Villa Carolina, Ltd"
                };

//
// Class 'custRec'
//
class custRec
{
        int recNum;                     // Record number
        char name[MAX_NAME];            // Customer name

    public:
        custRec();                      // Constructor
        ~custRec();                     // Destructor
        void *operator new    ( size_t ); // operator new
        void *operator new[]  ( size_t ); // operator new[]
        void operator delete  ( void* );  // operator delete
        void operator delete[]( void* );  // operator
                                          // delete[]

        void InitData( char *newName, int newRec );
        void ShowData();
};

// Constructor
custRec::custRec()
{
    TRACE( custRec  constructor );
}

// Destructor
custRec::~custRec()
{
    TRACE( custRec  destructor );
}
```

```cpp
// operator new()
void* custRec::operator new( size_t size )
{
    TRACE( operator new );
    return malloc( size );
}


// operator delete()
void  custRec::operator delete( void *p )
{
    TRACE( operator delete );
    free( p );
}


// operator new[]()
void* custRec::operator new[]( size_t size )
{
    TRACE( operator new[] );
    return malloc( size );
}


// operator delete[]()
void  custRec::operator delete[]( void *p )
{
    TRACE( operator delete[] );
    free( p );
}


// Initializes class' data
void  custRec::InitData( char *newName, int newRec )
{
    strcpy( name, newName );
    recNum = newRec;
}
```

```
// Displays class' data
void  custRec::ShowData()
{
    printf( "Customer Name: %s \t Customer Record#: %d \n",
                                        name, recNum );
}

int main( void )
{
    custRec *pCust;

    // Create a dynamic instance of 'custRec'
    pCust = new custRec;

    // Initialize and display data
    pCust->InitData( "Le Chaland, Ltd", 0 );
    pCust->ShowData();

    // Delete dynamic instance
    delete pCust;


    int arraySize=sizeof(custName)/sizeof(custName[0]);


    // Create a dynamic array of 'custRec's
    pCust = new custRec[arraySize];

    // Initialize and display data
    for( int i=0; i<arraySize; i++ )
        pCust[i].InitData( custName[i], i+1 );

    for( i=0; i<arraySize; i++ )
        pCust[i].ShowData();
```

```
// Delete dynamic array
delete []pCust;

return 0;
}
```

Use delete []ptr for Dynamic Arrays

Arrays cannot be safely deleted with the *delete* operator! You must use the *delete[]* operator for deleting any arrays, including character arrays.

ie.   char *p = new char[100];

// .. Use p ..

delete [] p;

Conversion Functions

Instances of a class can be converted to another type via *conversion constructors* or *cast operators*.

Conversion Constructors

If a constructor of a class A takes a single argument of type B, then it is said that B can be converted to A with *conversion by constructor*. In other words, the compiler can use class A constructor taking a B as its argument to create an A from a B. Here is an example:

```
/////////////////////////////////////////////////////////
// CONVCONS.CPP: Conversion by constructor...        //
```

```
//////////////////////////////////////////////////
#include <string.h>

class Record
{
    public:
        Record( char *newName );
        //
        // ...
        //
};

int main( void )
{
    //
    // The following calls 'Record::Record(char*) '
    // to convert "Mervin C." into a 'Record'.
    //
    Record customer = "Mervin C.";

    // ...
    return 0;
}
```

Cast Operators

You can define member functions that provide explicit conversion from a class type to another type. These routines are referred to as *cast operators* or *conversion routines*. They have the following syntax:

operator *newTypeName* ( );

The following rules apply to conversion routines:

- A conversion routine takes no argument.

- A conversion routine has no explicit return type specified (the type specified following the *operator* keyword is the implied return type).

- A conversion routine may be declared as virtual.

- A conversion routine is inherited.

The following sample illustrates a class *conversion routine*:

```
/////////////////////////////////////////////////////////
// CONVERSN.CPP: A Class Conversion Routine...        //
/////////////////////////////////////////////////////////
#include <stdio.h>

class Value
{
        int val;
    public:
        operator int();
};

Value::operator int()
{
    return val;
}

int main( void )
{
    Value v;

    //
    // Following calls Value::operator int();
    //                             vvvvvv
    printf( "Value is %d \n", (int)v );
    return 0;
}
```

Friends

Class access specifiers allow you to control whether functions outside of your class can access the class members. There may be a case, however, in which your design calls for a particular function or class to access the *private* or *protected* members. C++ allows you to specifically grant access to any members of your class to another class or function by using the *friend* keyword.

Friend Classes

You can grant the members of another class (*anotherClass*) full access to the *private* and *protected* members of your class (*myClass*) by including a *friend* declaration in your class definition.

```
class myClass
{
        friend class anotherClass;
};
```

Friend Functions

You can grant a regular function or a member function of another class full access to the *private* and *protected* members of your class by including a *friend* declaration in your class definition.

```
class  myClass
{
        friend  void otherClass::MemberFuncName(int);
        friend  void regularFuncName(double);
};
```

Rules about Friends

The following rules apply to *friend* declarations and *friendship* :

- *friend* declarations are not affected by the *public, protected,* or *private* keywords.

- *friend* declarations are not mutual: if *A* declares *B* as a friend, the declaration does not imply that *A* is also a friend of *B*.

- *friendship* is not inherited: if *A* declared *B* as a friend, classes derived from *B* do not have automatic access to *A*'s members.

- *friendship* is not transitive: if *A* declared *B* as a friend, classes derived from *A* do not automatically grant friendship to *B*.

Overloading Member Functions

Member functions of a class can be overloaded; two or more member functions may have the same name as long as their argument lists are different. The compiler takes care of calling the correct function based on the arguments passed. It is fairly common for *constructors* to be overloaded. The following example illustrates:

```
//////////////////////////////////////////////////////
// OVERLD.CPP: Overloaded member functions...        //
//////////////////////////////////////////////////////
#include <time.h>

const int TIME_STR_LEN = 30;

class Time
{
```

```
        char timeStr[TIME_STR_LEN];
    public:
        Time();
        Time( char *str );
};


int main( void )
{
    Time T1;                      // Calls Time::Time();

    time_t t;
    time( &t );
    Time T2( ctime( &t ) );       // Calls Time::Time(char*);

    // ...

    return 0;
}
```

Overloading Operators

C++ allows you to define and use operators with your class. This feature, referred to as *operator overloading*, allows your class to behave just like a built-in type. You can overload any of the following operators for your class:

Table 6.4 Operators That Can Be Overloaded

+	-	*	/	%	^	&	|	~
!	=	<	>	+=	-=	*=	/=	%=
^=	&=	|=	<<	>>	>>=	<<=	==	!=
<=	>=	&&	||	++	—	,	->*	->
()	[]							

The following operators cannot be overloaded:

.   .*   ::   ?:

Rules

The following rules apply to operator overloading and operator functions:

- The Operator of Precedence and Associativity rules applied to expressions with built-in data types remain unchanged when evaluating overloaded operator functions.

- An operator function cannot change the way an operator works with built-in data types.

- An operator function must either be a member function or take one or more arguments of a class type.

- An operator function cannot have default arguments.

- Except for *operator=( )*, operator functions are inherited.

Samples

The following examples illustrate overloading of the ! operator and the [] operator:

```cpp
/////////////////////////////////////////////////////
// OPEROVR1.CPP Overloading Operators...            //
/////////////////////////////////////////////////////
#include <string.h>
#include <stdio.h>

const int MAX_LEN=100;

//
// Class to store name...
//
class Name
{
        char data[MAX_LEN];
    public:
        Name();

        void  SetData( char *newData );
        int operator !();
};

//
// Constructor: initialize name to 0s
//
Name::Name()
{
    memset( data, '\0', sizeof(data) );
}

//
// Save new name specified
```

```
//
void Name::SetData( char *newData )
{
    strcpy( data, newData );
}


//
// Overload operator! (): returns whether there's data
//
int Name::operator!()
{
    return( data[0] == '\0' );
}



int main( void )
{
    Name name;

    if ( !name )        //  <-- Implicit call to operator! ()
        printf( "No data assigned yet!\n" );

    name.SetData( "Beau-Bassin" );

    // Now an explicit call to operator! ()
    if ( ! name.operator!() )
        printf( "Data assigned... \n" );

    return 0;
}

//////////////////////////////////////////////////////////
// OPEROVR2.CPP Overloading Operators...              //
//////////////////////////////////////////////////////////
#include <string.h>
```

```c
#include <stdio.h>

const int MAX_LEN=100;

//
// Class to store spy name + spy key
//
class SecretInfo
{
        int  decoderKey;
        char codeName[MAX_LEN];
    public:
        SecretInfo( char *_spyName, int _spyKey );
        int  operator []( const char *_spyName );
};

//
// Constructor: Save spy info...
//
SecretInfo::SecretInfo( char *_spyName, int _spyKey )
{
    strcpy( codeName, _spyName );
    decoderKey =  _spyKey;
}

//
// Subscript operator overloaded to take string as index!!
//
int SecretInfo::operator []( const char *_spyName )
{
    if ( !strcmp( codeName, _spyName ) )
        return decoderKey;
    else
        return 0;
}
```

```
int main( void )
{
    SecretInfo agent( "J. Bond", 7 );

    char temp[MAX_LEN];
    printf( "Enter your code name: " );
    gets( temp );

    if ( agent[temp] ) // Calls operator[]( const char* );
        printf( "Your decoder key is %03d",
                                agent.operator[]( temp ) );
    else
        printf( "Sorry Bond!, invalid code name." );

    return 0;
}
```

Static Members

You can declare a class data member or class member function as *static*. A *static* member of a class can be viewed as a global variable or function only accessible within the scope of the class.

Static Data Members

A data member declared as *static* is shared by all instances of the class: only one copy of the variable is allocated, regardless of the number of instances of the class that are created. Actually, the static data member is allocated even if no instances of the class exist. A class with a *static* data member must both *declare* and *define* the data member:

- Declaring a static data member:

```
class myClass
{
        static int count;
};
```

- Defining the static data member:

    int *myClass::*count = 0;

Static Member Functions

A static member function of a class is not associated with any particular instance of the class. In other words, it is not passed a *this* pointer when called. The following can result:

- A static member function may be called whether or not an instance of the class exists.

- A static member function can access only the *static* data members of the class and call other *static* member functions of the class.

- A static member function cannot be declared as *virtual*.

const Objects and const Member Functions

You can create an instance of a class with the *const* modifier. The *const* keyword informs the compiler that the contents of the object cannot be modified after it has been initialized. To prevent the values of a *const* object from being changed, the compiler generates an error if a *const* object is used with a non *const* member function.

The following applies to *const* member function:

- Declared with the keyword *const* following its parameter list

- May not modify the contents of the class's data members

- May not call non-*const* member functions

- Can be called for *const* and non-*const* objects

The following example illustrates const objects and const member functions:

```
////////////////////////////////////////////////////
// CONSTOBJ.CPP: const objects and member functions. //
////////////////////////////////////////////////////

class    Coord
{
        int x, y;
    public:
        Coord(int _x, int _y);
        void SetVal(int _x, int _y);
        void GetVal(int &x, int &y) const;
};
```

```
//
// Constructor
//
Coord::Coord(int _x, int _y)
{
    x = _x;
    y = _y;
}


//
// Set x & y values   / non-const member function
//
void Coord::SetVal(int _x, int _y)
{
    x = _x;
    y = _y;
}


//
// Gets x & y values / const member function
//
void Coord::GetVal( int &_x, int &_y) const
{
    _x = x;
    _y = y;
}


//
// main()
//
int main( void )
{
    Coord        c1(10, 10);
    const Coord c2(20, 20);
```

```
    int x, y;
    c1.GetVal(x, y);

    // Incorrect: calling non-const
    // function with const object
    // c2.SetVal(x, y);

    c2.GetVal(x, y);

    return 0;
}
```

Class Inheritance

C++ allows a class to *inherit* the data members and member functions of one or more other classes. In other words, a new class can acquire the attributes and behavior of an already existing class. The new class is referred to as a *derived* class. The class whose members are inherited by the *derived* class is known as a *base* class. A *derived* class can itself act as a *base* class for another class.

Inheritance or *derivation* allows you to encapsulate (abstract) some common and related behavior into a (base) class. Several classes can then inherit that behavior by deriving from the (base) class.

Inheritance also allows you to slightly modify the behavior of an existing class. A derived class may redefine one or more member functions of a base class while inheriting the bulk of the base class' behavior and attributes.

The syntax for inheritance is

```
class   base
{
        // ...
};
```

```
class derived : access_key base [,access_key base2, ...]
{
     // ...
};
```

The *access_key* is optional and can be *private, protected,* or *public*.
When not specified, the *access_key* defaults to *private* for classes and
public for structures.

Public, Protected, and Private Base Classes

In Inheritance, the *access_key* governs the *access* level of the members
of a *base* class within the *derived* class. The following table describes
each *access_key*:

Table 6.5 Public, Protected, and Private Derivation

Derivation	*Access in* base	*New Access in* derived
public:	public	public (unchanged)
	protected	protected (unchanged)
	private	private (unchanged)
protected:	public	protected
	protected	protected (unchanged)
	private	private (unchanged)
private:	public	private
	protected	private
	private	private (unchanged)

In the following example

- *B1* is a public base class of *Derived*.

- *B2* is a protected base class of *Derived*.

- *B3* is a private base class of *Derived*.

```
/////////////////////////////////////////////////////////
// BASECLASS.CPP: Base classes...                       //
/////////////////////////////////////////////////////////

class B1
{
    // ...
};

class B2
{
    // ...
};

class B3
{
    // ...
};

class Derived : public B1, protected B2, private B3
{
    // ...
}
```

Simple Inheritance

Simple Inheritance refers to the case in which a *derived* class has only
one *base* class. The following sample illustrates *simple inheritance*:

```
//////////////////////////////////////////////////////
// SIMPLEIN.CPP: Simple Inheritance...              //
//////////////////////////////////////////////////////
#include <stdio.h>
#include <conio.h>
#include <string.h>

const int MAX_LEN = 10;

//
```

```cpp
// Coord: encapsulates an x and y value.
//
class Coord
{
    protected:
        int x, y;
    public:
        Coord(int _x=0, int _y=0);
        void SetLoc(int _x, int _y);
};


//
// Coord, Constructor (Initializes Coordinates)
//
Coord::Coord(int _x, int _y)
{
    SetLoc(_x, _y);
}


//
// Coord::SetLoc: Update values of x and y
//
void Coord::SetLoc(int _x, int _y)
{
    x = _x;
    y = _y;
}


//
// MsgAtCoord: Encapsulates a message
//             Inherits from Coord...
//
class MsgAtCoord : public Coord
{
        char msg[MAX_LEN];
    public:
```

```cpp
        MsgAtCoord( char *_msg = "NO MSG" );
        void SetMsg(char *_msg);
        void Show();
};


//
// MsgAtCoord: constructor
//
MsgAtCoord::MsgAtCoord( char *_msg)
{
    SetMsg( _msg );
}


//
// MsgAtCoord::SetMsg, updates message
//
void MsgAtCoord::SetMsg( char *_msg)
{
    strcpy( msg, _msg );
}


//
// MsgAtCoord::Show, displays message at x, y
//
void MsgAtCoord::Show()
{
    gotoxy(x, y);
    printf( msg );
}


//
// main: Creates and execises MsgAtCoord
//
int main( void )
{
    MsgAtCoord greeting;
```

```
greeting.SetLoc( 10, 10 );
greeting.SetMsg( "Hello..." );
greeting.Show();

return 0;
}
```

Using the IDE's Browser To View Class Hierarchies

The IDE has a browser that represents the hierarchy of classes in a visual form. Figure 6.1 shows one of the ways the *Browser* represents the classes from the *simple inheritance* example:

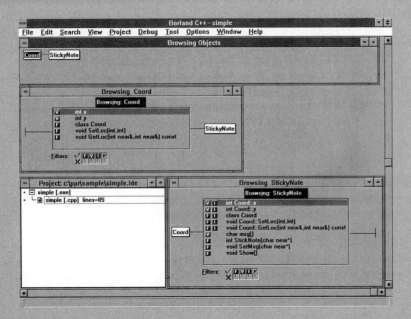

Figure 6.1. *IDE's Class Browser.*

Constructors and Destructors in Inheritance

Constructors are not inherited. If the constructor of a base class expects one or more parameters, the constructor of the derived class must call the base class constructor with the necessary parameters from the *member initialization list*.

```
///////////////////////////////////////////////////////
// CTR_BASE.CPP: Constructor and Inheritance...        //
///////////////////////////////////////////////////////
#include <string.h>

class Base
{
    public:
        Base(int, float);
};


class Derived : public Base
{
    public:
        Derived( char *lst, float=1.00000 );
};


Derived::Derived( char *lst, float amt ) : Base( strlen(lst),
amt )
{
}
```

On the other hand, the destructor of a derived class does not need to explicitly call the destructor of a base class. The compiler automically generates a call to base destructors within the derived's destructor.

Virtual Functions

A member function can be declared as *virtual*. The *virtual* keyword instructs the compiler to generate some additional information about the function. If the function is redefined in a derived class and called with a base class pointer (or reference) that points to (or aliases) an instance of the derived class, the information allows the correct version of the function to be called: the call invokes the derived class version of the function.

The following example illustrates the difference between a *virtual* and a *non-virtual* function:

```
///////////////////////////////////////////////////
// VIRTUAL.CPP: Using Virtual Member Functions...    //
///////////////////////////////////////////////////
#include <stdio.h>

//
// Base class with one virtual
// and one non-virtual function
//
class Base
{
    public:
        virtual void virt()
        {
            printf( "Hello from Base::virt \n" );
        }
```

```cpp
        void  nonVirt()
        {
            printf( "Hello from Base::nonVirt \n" );
        }
};


//
// Derived class: Overrides both functions
//                from Base class...
//
class Derived : public Base
{
    public:
        void virt()
        {
            printf( "Hello from Derived::virt \n" );
        }
        void  nonVirt()
        {
            printf( "Hello from Derived::nonVirt \n" );
        }
};


//
// main function
//
int main( void )
{
    Base *bp = new Derived;     // Base pointer really
                                // pointing to derived instance
```

```
bp->virt();        // Call virtual function
bp->nonVirt();     // Call non-virtual function

return 0;
}
```

Figure 6.2. *Output of the VIRTUAL.CPP sample*

The results of the preceding program reveal that in the case of the virtual function, the derived version of the function was correctly called. The call to the *nonVirt* (non-virtual) function, however, invoked *Base::nonVirt* although the object was really a *derived* object.

The Virtual Mechanism Requires Pointers or References

To invoke the virtual mechanism you must use pointers or references. Only a class pointer (or reference) can point (alias) an instance of a derived class.

The following rules apply to virtual functions:

- A *virtual* function cannot be declared as *static*.

- The *virtual* specifier is optional when overriding a virtual function in a derived class.

- A *virtual* function must be defined or declared pure.

Disabling the Virtual Mechanism

You can disable the virtual mechanism by specifying a class name and the scope resolution operator when invoking a virtual function.

```cpp
/////////////////////////////////////////////////////
// NO_VIRT.CPP: Disabling the virtual mechanism...   //
/////////////////////////////////////////////////////
#include <stdio.h>

class Base
{
    public:
        virtual void virt()
        { printf( "Hello from Base::virt \n" ); }
};

class Derived : public Base
{
    public:
        void virt()
        { printf( "Hello from Derived::virt \n" ); }
};

int main( void )
{
    Base *bp = new Derived;         // Base pointer really
                                    // pointing to derived in-
stance
    bp->virt();                     // Uses virtual mechanism
    bp->Base::virt();               // Disables virtual mechanism

    return 0;
}
```

Implementation

Virtual functions are implemented with a *jump table*. The following outlines the implemetation:

- For each class containing virtual functions, the compiler builds a table that contains the address of these functions. The table is commonly referred to as the *virtual method table* or *vtable*.

- Each instance of a class with virtual functions contains a (hidden) pointer to its *virtual method table*. This pointer is commonly known as the *virtual method pointer, virtual table pointer,* or *vptr*.

- The compiler automatically inserts a snippet of code at the beginning of the constructor of the class. The code initializes a class's *virtual table pointer*.

- For any given hierarchy, the address of a particular *virtual* function is stored at the same offset within the *virtual method table*s of each class.

- When you call a virtual function, the code generated by the compiler first retrieves the *virtual table pointer*. Next, the code accesses the *virtual method table* to retrieve the address of the *virtual* function. Then the code executes an indirect call to the function.

Polymorphism and Late Binding

Two terms commonly used when referring to C++ inheritance and virtual functions are *polymorphism* and *Late (dynamic) Binding*.

Polymorphism is the ability of a base class to propose or supply an interface of virtual functions that can be reimplemented by several classes deriving from the base class. In other words, it is the capability of a base class pointer or reference to "*assume various forms, characters, or styles*" (Webster's definition of *polymorphic*) with inheritance and virtual functions.

Late Binding refers to the fact that the compiler cannot determine the actual function called when a virtual function is invoked with a pointer or reference to a base class. Although defined as a base class pointer, the variable could actually be pointing to an instance of a derived class. Given the implementation of the virtual mechanism, the address of the function can be evaluated only at run time.

Use Virtual Destructor in Base Classes

Consider the following setup:

```cpp
class Base
{
    public:
        ~Base()
        {
            // Cleanup
        }
};

class Derived : public Base
{
    public:
        ~Derived()
        {
            // Cleanup
        }
};

int main( void )
{
    Base *bp = new Derived;
    // ...
    delete bp;

    return 0;
}
```

Because the destructor is not virtual, the call to *operator delete* will call only *Base::~Base* possibly resulting in the loss of resources used by *Derived*. By making *Base::~Base* virtual, the appropriate destructor is called instead.

Multiple Inheritance

C++ supports *multiple inheritance*: that is, a class is derived from more than one base class. This feature allows you to combine the behavior of several classes into one class. The following example illustrates this technique. The class *Coord* keeps tracks of *x/y* values. The class *Message* keeps track of a message. By deriving from both *Coord* and *Message*, the class *MessageXY* inherits the capability to keep track of both *x/y* values and a message. The new class simply adds a *Show* member function to display the message at location x/y:

```
/////////////////////////////////////////////////////
// SIMPLEIN.CPP: Simple Inheritance...               //
/////////////////////////////////////////////////////
#include <stdio.h>
#include <conio.h>
#include <string.h>

const int MAX_LEN = 10;

//
// Coord: encapsulates an x and y value.
//
class Coord
{
    protected:
        int x, y;
```

```cpp
    public:
        Coord(int _x=0, int _y=0);
        void SetLoc(int  _x, int  _y);
};


//
// Coord, Constructor (Initializes Coordinates)
//
Coord::Coord(int _x, int _y)
{
    SetLoc(_x, _y);
}


//
// Coord::SetLoc: Update values of x and y
//
void Coord::SetLoc(int _x, int _y)
{
    x = _x;
    y = _y;
}


//
// class Message : stores a string
//
class Message
{
    protected:
        char msg[MAX_LEN];

    public:
        void SetMsg(char *_msg)
        {
            strcpy( msg, _msg );
        }
};
```

```cpp
//
// class MessageXY : Inherits from Coord and
//                   Message...
//
class MessageXY : public Coord, public Message
{
    public:
        void Show();
};


//
// MessageXY::Show, displays message at current location
//
void MessageXY::Show()
{
    gotoxy(x, y);
    printf( msg );
}


//
//
// main: Creates and exercises MessageXY
//
int main( void )
{
    MessageXY greeting;

    greeting.SetLoc( 10, 10 );
    greeting.SetMsg( "Hello..." );
    greeting.Show();

    return 0;
}
```

Ambiguity and Scope Resolution

In a hierarchy with multiple inheritance, a class may indirectly inherit two copies of a base.

```cpp
///////////////////////////////////////////////////
// AMBIG.CPP: Ambiguity in Multiple Inheritance...   //
///////////////////////////////////////////////////
class A
{
    protected:
        int  data;
    public:
        void func()
        {
            // ...
        }
};

class B : public A
{
    // ...
};

class C : public A
{
    // ...
};

class D : public B, public C
{
    // ...
};

int main( void )
{
```

```
    D d;

    d.func();
    d.data - 10;

    return 0;
}
```

In the preceding sample code, the call to the function f( ) in *main* generates the following error:

```
Error ambig.cpp 34: Member is ambiguous: 'A::func' and 'A::func'
in function main()
```

```
Error ambig.cpp 35: Member is ambiguous: 'A::data' and 'A::data'
in function main()
```

```
*** 2 errors in Compile ***
```

You can resolve ambiguity conflicts by using the *scope resolution operator*. For example, replace *d.func( )* with *d.B::func( )* [or *d.C::func( )*]
and replace *d.data* with *d.B::data* [or *d.C::data*] to eliminate the error
messages.

Virtual Base Class

Although the *scope resultion operator* provides a workaround for member function and data ambiguities in multiple inheritance, you may still
want to ensure that your derived class inherits only one copy of a
particuar base class. You can achieve this goal by adding the keyword
virtual when deriving from the base class. The following sample is a
modified version of the AMBIG.CPP file with class *A* as a *virtual base
class*:

```
/////////////////////////////////////////////////////
// VIRTBASE.CPP: Virtual Base Class Sample...        //
/////////////////////////////////////////////////////
```

```
class A
{
    protected:
        int   data;

    public:
        void func()
        {
            // ...
        }
};

class B : virtual public A       // A's a virtual base class
{
    // ...
};

class C : virtual public A       // A's a virtual base class
{
    // ...
};

class D : public B, public C     // D has only one copy of A
{
    // ...
};

int main( void )
{
    D d;

    d.func();
    // d.data = 10; data is not accessible

    return 0;
}
```

The following list describes the order of construction of a derived class:

1. The base class constructor is called.

2. The constructors of data members, which are class objects, are called in the order that the objects are declared within the class.

3. The body of the derived's class constructor is executed.

The destruction of a derived class is executed in the reverse order of the class construction:

1. The destructor of the class is executed.

2. The destructors of data members, which are class objects, are called.

3. The destructor of the base class is called.

Abstract Classes and Pure Virtual Functions

An *abstract class* is a class that can be used only as a base class for other classes. An *abstract class* contains one or more *pure virtual functions*. A *pure virtual function* can be regarded as an inline function whose body is defined as *=0* (*the pure specifier*). You do not have to provide an actual definition for a *pure virtual function*: it is simply expected to be redefined in derived classes.

The following rules apply to *abstract classes*:

- An abstract class may not be used as an argument type or as a function return type.

- An abstract type may not be used in an explicit conversion.

- An instance of an abstract class (local/global variable or member data) may not be declared.

- A pointer or reference to an abstract class may be declared.

- If a class derived from an abstract class does not define all the *pure virtual* functions of the base class, the derived class is also an *abstract* class.

```
///////////////////////////////////////////////////
// ABSTRACT.CPP: Sample using abstract class....    //
///////////////////////////////////////////////////


//
// Bird is an abstract class with a pure
// virtual function Sing().
//
class Bird
{
    public:
        void virtual Sing() = 0;    //Pure virtual function
};



//
// Eagle is also an abstract class since
// it does not define Bird's pure virtual function
//
class Eagle : public Bird
{
};



//
// GoldenEagle defines the pure virtual function(s)
// of its base class. Hence it can be instantiated.
//
```

```
class GoldenEagle : public Eagle
{
    void Sing()
    {
        // ...
    }
};
```

Summary

A C++ program may not use all the object-oriented features presented in this chapter. There will be times, however, when a particular aspect of the language offers what seems to be the ideal means to represent and solve a problem. In the following chapter, you'll see how some of these features are applied in the C++ Input/Output stream library.

Chapter 7
The C++ Stream Classes

The C++ *iostream* library (C++ stream library) provides a group of classes for handling I/O. These classes offer several advantages over the traditional C I/O functions:

- Type-safety. The *printf* and *scanf* families of functions do not provide any type checking. A mismatch between the string specifier and the arguments provided cannot be flagged by the compiler. The C++ mechanism relies on *function (operator) overloading* to ensure that the proper function is called for the supplied data type.

- Extensibility. The C I/O routines are restricted to file streams (and some devices that are accessible as *predefined streams*). They do not allow for extensions. With the C++ classes, *polymorphism* can be applied to allow the same routines to act on different types of streams. For example, the same interface used for standard I/O is available for file I/O and in-memory I/O. You also can provide overloaded functions that allow the C++ streams library to use your own defined types.

- Simplicity and consistency. By making heavy use of overloaded functions, the stream library provides a uniform interface to I/O. This interface enhances the readiliy of your code and allows for better data abstraction. The I/O classes also rely on overloaded operators, which results in a simpler and more intuitive syntax.

This chapter offers a practical overview of the C++ stream library along with examples of its commonly used functions.

IOStream Header Files

To access the classes and functions of the C++ stream library from your program, you must include the *iostream.h* header file. You also may need to include *fstream.h* (File I/O), *iomanip.h* (Manipulators), and *strstream.h* (In-Memory I/O).

Predefined Stream Objects

The iostream library provides four predefined stream objects. They are associated with standard input and output. Table 7.1 describes the objects:

Table 7.1 Predefined C++ Stream Objects

Name	Class Type	Description
cin	istream_withassign	Associated with standard input (i.e. keyboard)
cout	ostream_withassign	Associated with standard output (i.e. screen)
cerr	ostream_withassign	Associated with the standard error device (i.e. screen) with unbuffered output
clog	ostream_withassign	Associated with the standard error device (i.e. screen) with buffered output.

Redirecting Input or Output

You can reassign *cin* or *cout* to your own stream objects. Reassigning them enables your program to easily redirect standard input or output. The following example illustrates:

```
////////////////////////////////////////////////////////
// REDIR.CPP: Redirecting standard streams...          //
////////////////////////////////////////////////////////
#include <iostream.h>
#include <fstream.h>

const int MAX_LINE = 80;

//
// Redirected input stream
//
ifstream ifs;

int main( int argc, char *argv[] )
{
    // If argument...
    if ( argc > 1 )
    {
        //  Attempt to open file
        ifs.open( argv[1] );

        // if successful, redirect input
        if ( ifs )
            cin = ifs;
    }

    // Prompt for input...
    cout << "Enter a line of text : ";
```

```
    // Read data from standard input
    char line[MAX_LINE];
    cin.getline( line, sizeof(line) );

    // Display data entered...
    cout << endl << "You've entered: " << line;

    return 0;
}
```

Insertion and Extraction Operators

The C++ stream library provides two basic classes for input and output: *istream* and *ostream*, respectively. The *ostream* class uses the left-shift operator (<<) for ouput. When used with C++ stream objects, this operator is referred to as the *insertion* operator. The following example displays a greeting using the *insertion* operator with the predefined *cout* object:

```
#include <iostream.h>
int main( void )
{
    cout << "Hello! ";
    return 0;
}
```

The *istream* class uses the right-shift operator (>>) for input. Used in that context, the operator is often referred to as the *extraction* operator. The following example uses the predefined *cin* object and the *extraction* operator to read a string from the keyboard:

```
#inlcude <iostream.h>

int  main( void )
{
    char name[100];

    cout << "Please enter your name: ";
    cin  >> name;
    cout << "Hello ";
    cout << name;
    return 0;
}
```

Operators Overloaded for Built-In Types

The *istream* and *ostream* classes overload the *extraction* and *insertion* operators, respectively, for all the built-in types. This overload enables you to use a consistent syntax to output and input characters, integers, real numbers, and strings. The following example illustrates the uniform syntax available for outputting variables of different types:

```
///////////////////////////////////////////////////
// COUT.CPP: Illustrates built-in type stream support//
///////////////////////////////////////////////////
#include <iostream.h>


int main( void )
{
    char         c = 'A';
    signed char  sc= 'B';
```

```
unsigned char uc= 'C';
int           i = 0xd;
float         f = 1.7;
double        d = 2.8;

cout << c;     // calls operator << (          char)
cout << sc;    // calls operator << (   signed char)
cout << uc;    // calls operator << (unsigned char)
cout << i;     // calls operator << ( int )
cout << f;     // calls operator << ( float )
cout << d;     // calls operator << ( double)

return 0;
}
```

Inline Versions of Functions

Several of the functions in the IOStream library (including some overloaded insertion and extraction operators) are defined inline in the file *iostream.h*. However, they are not available unless the macro _BIG_INLINE is defined. If you need additional performance and do not mind the increase in size, you can define this macro before including iostream.h.

Chaining Operator Calls

The overloaded << and >> operators of *istream* and *ostream* return a reference to an object of their respective type. This reference enables you to chain several operator calls together. Therefore, the prior example using *cout* can be simplified as follows:

```
/////////////////////////////////////////////////////
// COUT.CPP: Illustrates built-in type stream support//
/////////////////////////////////////////////////////
#include <iostream.h>


int main( void )
{
    char          c = 'A';
    signed char   sc= 'B';
    unsigned char uc= 'C';
    int           i = 0xd;
    float         f = 1.7;
    double        d = 2.8;

    cout  << c << sc << uc << i << f <<  d;

    return 0;
}
```

Adding Stream Support for User-Defined Types

You easily can extend the iostream library to support your own types with the *insertion* and *extraction* operators. You must define two functions with the following signatures:

```
// Reading data from stream
istream& operator >> ( istream& is, MyType &varName );

// Writing data to stream
ostream& operator << ( ostream& os, MyType &varName );
```

The following example illustrates:

```
///////////////////////////////////////////////////
// IO4TYPE.CPP: Providing I/O support for user type  //
///////////////////////////////////////////////////

#include <iostream.h>
#include <assert.h>


struct  NewType
{
    int x;
    int y;
};



//
// Read: expecting format '(##,##)'
//
istream&  operator >> ( istream &is, NewType &nt )
{
    char c;

    cin >>  c;
    assert( c == '(' );

    cin >> nt.x;

    cin >>  c;
    assert( c == ',' );

    cin >>  nt.y;

    cin >>  c;
    assert( c == ')' );

    return is;
}
```

```
//
// Write: use '(##,##)' format
//
ostream&  operator << ( ostream &os, NewType &nt )
{
    os << '('
        << nt.x
        << ','
        << nt.y
        << ')';

    return os;
}


int main( void )
{
    cout << "Enter two numbers: ";

    int  ix;
    cin  >> ix;

    int  iy;
    cin  >> iy;

    NewType nt;
    nt.x = ix;
    nt.y = iy;

    cout << "Value entered :"
         << nt
         << endl;

    return 0;
}
```

Declare Insertion and Extraction Operators as Friends

When using classes, it is common to declare the insertion and extraction operators as friends of your class. This declaration enables the operator access to the private data members of your class when formatting input or output:

```
/////////////////////////////////////////////////////////
// IO_TYPE.CPP: iostream support of user-types...     //
/////////////////////////////////////////////////////////

#include <iostream.h>


class TPiece
{
        // .. ( Private Data )

    public:
        //
        // ...
        //
    friend istream& operator >> ( istream&, TPiece& );
    friend ostream& operator << ( ostream&, const TPiece& );
};



//
// Provides stream output support
//
ostream&  operator << ( ostream &os, const TPiece &p )
{
    //
    // ... ( Can access private Data for formatting )
    //
    return os;
}
```

continues

continued

```
//
// etc.
//
```

Formatting

The C++ stream library provides three ways to control the format of data: *formatting member functions*, using *flags*, and using *manipulators*. The following section describes each method with illustrative examples.

Formatting Member Functions

The members functions provided by the class *ios* for formatting purposes are overloaded to allow a control attribute to be read or set. Also the C++ stream library often provides *manipulators* for the attributes that can be controlled via member functions. The following section describes the attributes for which the *ios* class provides functions.

Field Width

The class *ios* provides the *width* function to read and set a stream's field width, as shown in table 7.2.

Table 7.2 *width* Method of Class *ios*

Function	Description
int ios::width();	Returns the current value of the stream's width variable
int ios::width(int);	Sets the stream's internal field width variable.

Additional Information:

- When used with input, the *width* method can be used to set the maximum number of characters to be read in.

- When used with output, the *width* method specifies the minimum field width.

- If the field is less than the specified width, the output is padded with the stream's *fill* character.

- If the output is larger than the specified width, the *width* value is ignored.

- The default *width* is 0 (the output is neither truncated nor padded).

- The *width* is reset to 0 after each insertion.

- Note the related *setw* manipulator.

The following sample illustrates how to use *width* to limit the number of characters read in during input:

```
//////////////////////////////////////////////////
// WIDTH1.CPP: Using ios::width with input...      //
//////////////////////////////////////////////////
#include <iostream.h>
```

```cpp
const int MAX_LEN=10;

int main( void )
{
    char name[MAX_LEN];

    // Prompt for user's name
    cout << "Please enter name "
         << "(max " << MAX_LEN-1    // minus 1 for '\0';
         << " chars) :";

    // Set maximum width
    cin.width( MAX_LEN );

    // Read name
    cin >> name;

    // Greet user
    cout << "Hello " << name << '!';

    return 0;
}
```

The next example uses the *width* function to right justify numbers:

```cpp
/////////////////////////////////////////////////////
// WIDTH2.CPP: Using ios::width with output..        //
/////////////////////////////////////////////////////
#include <iostream.h>

const int FLD_WIDTH=10;

int main( void )
{
    int x1 =  2867;
    int y1 = 20051;
```

```
int z1 =    017;

cout.width(FLD_WIDTH);
cout << x1   << '\n';

cout.width(FLD_WIDTH);
cout << y1   << '\n';

cout.width(FLD_WIDTH);
cout << z1   << '\n';

return 0;
}
```

Padding Character

The *ios::fill* functions can be used to read the current padding (fill) character or to set a new one (see table 7.3).

Table 7.3 *fill* Method of Class *ios*

Function	Description
char ios::fill();	Returns the stream's fill (padding) character
char ios::fill(char);	Sets the stream's internal fill character and returns the previous value

Additional Information:

- The default *fill* character is a space.

- Note the related *setfill* manipulator.

The following example uses the *fill* method to zero pad numbers:

```
///////////////////////////////////////////////////////
// FILL.CPP: Using ios::fill...                        //
///////////////////////////////////////////////////////
#include <iostream.h>

// Field width constant
const int  FLD_WIDTH= 10;

// Fill char constant
const char FILL_CHAR= '0';

int main( void )
{
    int x1 =  2867;
    int y1 = 20051;

    cout.fill(FILL_CHAR);

    cout.width(FLD_WIDTH);
    cout << x1  << '\n';

    cout.width(FLD_WIDTH);
    cout << y1  << '\n';

    return 0;
}
```

Digits of Floating Point Precision

The *ios::precison* functions can be used to read the current number of significant digits or to set the significant decimal digits used when displaying floating-point numbers (see table 7.4).

Table 7.4 *precision* Method of Class *ios*

Function	Description
int ios::precision(int);	Sets the stream internal floating-point precision variable and returns the previous value
int ios::precision();	Returns the stream's precision value

Additional Information:

- The default precision is six digits.

- If the *scientific* or the *fixed* flag is set, *precision* controls the number of digits displayed after the decimal point.

- If neither the *scientific* nor the *fixed* flag is set, *precision* controls the total number of significant digits.

- Note the related *setprecision* manipulator.

The following example illustrates the use of *precision*:

```
/////////////////////////////////////////////////////
// PRECISN.CPP: Using ios::precision...            //
/////////////////////////////////////////////////////
#include <iostream.h>

int main( void )
{
    float  f = 3456.141592;
    double d = 50.2345639101;

    cout.precision( 4 );
    cout << d  << '\n';      // displays 50.23

    cout << f  << '\n';      // displays 3456
```

```
    cout.precision( 3 );
    cout << f  << '\n';      // displays 3.46e+03

    // set the fixed flag
    cout.setf( ios::fixed, ios::floatfield );

    cout << f  << '\n';      // displays 34563.142

    return 0;
}
```

Formatting Flags

C++ streams support *format flags*. They control how input and output are formatted. The flags are *bit-fields* stored in a *long* variable. The class *ios* provides the functions shown in table 7.5 to manipulate a stream's format flags.

Table 7.5 Method To Manipulate a Stream's Format Flags

Function	Description
long ios::flags();	Returns stream's current flags
long ios::flags(long);	Sets the stream's flags to the parameter specified and returns the previous value of the flags
long ios::setf(long,long);	Sets the values of the flags whose bits are on in the second parameter to the value of the corresponding bits in the first parameter. It returns the previous value of all flags.

Function	Description
long ios::setf(long);	Sets the flags whose bits are set on in the specified parameter; returns the previous value of all flags
long ios::unsetf(long);	Clears the flags whose bits are on in the specified parameter. It returns the value of all the flags.

The following table describes the format flags:

Table 7.6 Format Flags of *ios*

Flag	Default	Description
ios::skipws	X	If set, leading white space is ignored on input.
ios::left		If set, data is left justified on output.
ios::right	X	If set or if ios::left and ios::internal are not set, data is right justified on output.
ios::internal		If set, the sign of a number is left justified, and the number is right justified. The area between is padded with the *fill* character.
ios::dec	X	If set, numbers are displayed in base 10 (decimal).
ios::oct		If set, numbers are displayed in base 8 (octal).
ios::hex		If set, numbers are displayed in base 16 (hexadecimal).

continues

Chapter 7: The C++ Stream Classes **265**

Table 7.6 continued

Flag	Default	Description
ios::showbase		If set, the C/C++ base indicators ("0x" for hex and "0" for octal numbers) is inserted for numeric output.
ios::showpoint		If set, the decimal point is displayed with outputting floats, doubles, and long doubles.
ios::uppercase		If set, the letters A through F of hexademical numbers are uppercased. The E of scientific numbers is also uppercased.
ios::showpos		If set, the + sign is output for positive values.
ios::scientific		If set, real numbers are displayed using scientific notatation (i.e. n.xxxEy, 1.2345e2).
ios::fixed		If set, real numbers are displayed using fixed notation (i.e. nnn.ddd, 123.45).
ios::unitbuf		If set, the stream is flushed after every insertion.
ios::stdio		If set, *stdout* and *stderr* are flush after every insertion.

Additional Information:

- ios::left, ios::right, and ios::internal are mutually exclusive. Only one can be set at any time.

- ios::dec, ios::oct, and ios::hex are mutually exclusive. Only one can be set at any time.

- The constant *ios::basefield* can be used as second parameter to *setf* when modifying the base.

- The constant *ios::adjustfield* can be used as second parameter to *setf* when setting the field adjustment.

- The constant *ios::floatfield* can be used as second parameter to *setf* when setting the floating point notation.

The following examples illustrate the various flags.

```
///////////////////////////////////////////////////
// FLAGS1.CPP: Using iostream formatting flags...    //
///////////////////////////////////////////////////
#include <iostream.h>
#include <limits.h>

int main( void )
{
    int i = 0;

    // Prompt user for number...
    cout << "Enter an integer with optional "
            "leading whitespace: ";

    // This read will skip white space
    cin  >> i;

    // Display info to user...
    cout << "You've entered " << i << endl;

    // Remove char. in input stream
    cin.ignore( INT_MAX, '\n' );
```

```cpp
    // Prompt user again
    cout << "Enter an integer with optional "
            "leading whitespace: ";

    // Clear skip-whitespace flag
    cin.unsetf( ios::skipws );

    // This read will NOT skip white space.
    cin >> i;

    // Check if input had white space [or just incorrect
    // values] and inform user...
    cin.good() ? (cout << "You've entered " << i << endl):
                 (cout << "Incorrect input..."   << endl);

    return 0;
}



/////////////////////////////////////////////////////
// FLAGS2.CPP: Using iostream formatting flags...    //
/////////////////////////////////////////////////////
#include <iostream.h>


int main( void )
{
    int x = 1678;

    // Display value
    cout << "Value of x = " << x << '\n';

    // Save original flags
    long savedFlags = cout.flags();
```

```cpp
    // Enable base indicator and hex base
    cout.setf( ios::showbase | ios::hex );

    // Display value again
    cout << "Value of x = " << x << '\n';

    return 0;
}



//////////////////////////////////////////////////////////
// FLAGS3.CPP: Using iostream formatting flags...      //
//////////////////////////////////////////////////////////
#include <iostream.h>


int main( void )
{
    float   f = 2.3456789e6;
    double  d = 3.0e9;

    // Display values
    cout << "Value of f = " << f << '\n';
    cout << "Value of d = " << d << '\n';

    // Show '+' signs for +ve numbers
    cout.setf( ios::showpos );

    // Set fixed notation;
    cout.setf( ios::fixed, ios::floatfield );

    // Display values again
    cout << "Value of f = " << f << '\n';
    cout << "Value of d = " << d << '\n';

    return 0;
}
```

Manipulators

Manipulators are functions that can be included right in the middle of chained insertion or extraction expressions. They provide a convenient way to modify the format flags of a stream. However, manipulators are not limited to modifying the format of I/O. Except for *setw*, the changes performed by manipulators are permanent until reset.

Simple Manipulators

Manipulators that do not take any arguments are referred to as *simple* manipulators. Table 7.7 describes the predefined simple manipulators.

Table 7.7 Simple Manipulators

Manipulator	Description
endl	Inserts a new-line character (\n) into an output stream and then calls the *flush* manipulator
ends	Inserts a null character (\0) into an output stream. It is commonly used to terminate a string
flush	Forces all output to be written to their respective physical devices
dec	Sets the conversion base to decimal (see ios::dec)
hex	Sets the conversion base to hexadecimal (see ios::hex)
oct	Sets the conversion base to octal (see ios::oct)
ws	Causes leading white space to be ignored on input (see ios::skipws)

The following example illustrates the use of simple manipulators:

```cpp
////////////////////////////////////////////////////////
// MANIP1.CPP: Using simple predefined manipulators. //
////////////////////////////////////////////////////////

#include <iostream.h>
#include <iomanip.h>

int main( void )
{
    int i;

    // Prompt for input
    cout << "Please enter a number :";

    // Extract number
    cin >> i;

    // Check for incorrect entry
    if ( !cin )
    {
        // Inform user of error...
        cout << "Invalid input..." << endl;
    }
    else
    {
        // Use hex, oct and dec manipulator
        //
        cout << "Hex: " << hex << i << endl
             << "Oct: " << oct << i << endl
             << "Dec: " << dec << i << endl;
    }

    return 0;
}
```

Parametized Manipulators

Parametized manipulators expect arguments. Table 7.8 describes the predefined parametized manipulators.

Table 7.8 Parametized Manipulators

Manipulator	*Description*
setbase(int _b);	Sets the conversion base according to the parameter specified:

Parameter	Conversion Base
0	Default base: • Input uses decimal except for numbers octal and hexdecimal, respectively. • Output uses decimal.
8	I/O use octal base.
10	I/O use decimal base.
16	I/O use hexadecimal base.

resetiosflags(long _b);	Clears the flags whose corresponding bits are enabled in the passed parameter.
setiosflags(long _b);	Sets the flags whose corresponding bits are enabled in the passed parameter.
setfill(int _f);	Sets the fill character to the specified parameter.
setprecision(int _n);	Sets the stream's internal floating-point precision variable.

Manipulator	Description
setw(int _w);	Sets the stream's internal field width variable to the specified number:

- When used with input, the manipulator sets the maximum number of characters to be read in.

- When used with output, the manipulator specifies the minimum field width.

- If the field is less than the specified width, the output is padded with the stream's *fill* character.

- If the next output is larger than the specified width, width is ignored.

- The width is reset to 0 after each extraction or insertion.

The following example illustrates parametized manipulators:

```
////////////////////////////////////////////////////
// MANIP2.CPP: Using parametized manipulators.     //
////////////////////////////////////////////////////

#include <iostream.h>
#include <iomanip.h>

int main( void )
{
    double dbls[] = {
                    1.245,
                   -12.99133,
                  134.007804,
                   -2.345,
                    0.000003
                };
```

```
cout  << setfill( '.' )
      << setprecision( 4 )
      << setiosflags( ios::showpoint |
                      ios::fixed     |
                      ios::right     );

for (int i=0; i<sizeof(dbls)/sizeof(dbls[0]); i++)
    cout << "Result"
         << setw(20)
         << dbls[i]
         << endl;

    return 0;
}
```

Stream Errors

All stream objects are derived from the class *ios* and inherit a *state* data member. This member maintains the status of the stream in a collection of bits. The flags representing the possible states of the stream are enumerated in the *ios* class defined in the header file *iostream.h*:

```
class _EXPCLASS ios {
public:
    // stream status bits
    enum io_state   {
        goodbit  = 0x00,    // no bit set: all is ok
        eofbit   = 0x01,    // at end of file
        failbit  = 0x02,    // last I/O operation failed
        badbit   = 0x04,    // invalid operation attempted
        hardfail = 0x80     // unrecoverable error
        };
```

```
    // ...
    // ...
    // ...
};
```

Table 7.9 describes the status bits.

Table 7.9 Stream Error States

Enumerator	Description
ios::goodbit	Everything's OK.
ios::eofbit	Indicates that the end of the file has been reached.
ios::failbit	Indicates a formatting or conversion error: for example, data read was in an unexpected format. The stream is still usable (after the *failbit* is cleared).
ios::badbit	Indicates a serious error usually related with buffer operations: for example, a failure to extract characters, an attempt to seek past the end of the file, or an error while storing characters to the stream's buffer. The stream is probably no longer usable.
ios::hardfail	Indicates an unrecoverable error usually associated with hardware failure.

Querying and Setting a Stream's State

There are several functions and operators that enable you to read a stream's state. There also are functions to set or to clear a stream's state. Table 7.10 provides a brief description.

Table 7.10 Methods To Query a Stream's Status

Method	Description
int rdstate();	Returns the current state.
int eof();	Returns a nonzero value if the ios::eofbit flag is set.
int fail();	Returns a nonzero value if ios::failbit, ios::badbit, or ios::hardfail is set.
int bad();	Returns a nonzero value if ios::badbit or ios::hardfail is set.
int good();	Returns a nonzero value if all the error bits are clear.
void clear(int=0);	If the parameter is 0 (default), all bits are cleared. Otherwise, the parameter is stored as the error state.
operator void*();	Returns a null pointer if ios::failbit, ios::badbit, or ios::hardbit is set. (same as fail()).
int operator!();	Returns a nonzero value if ios::failbit, ios::badbit, or ios::hardfail is set. (same as fail()).

Common Manipulation of a Stream's State

Table 7.11 provides a summary of the common operations you can perform with a stream's *io_state* flags.

Table 7.11 io_state Flags Operations

Operation	Sample
Check whether *flag* is set:	if (*strm*.rdstate( ) & ios::*flag*)
Clear *flag*:	strm.clear(rdstate( ) & ~ios::*flag*)
Set *flag*:	strm.clear(rdstate( ) I ios::*flag*)
Set *flag*:	strm.clear(ios::*flag*) (reset other flags)
Clear all flags:	strm.clear( )

File I/O with C++ Streams

The C++ library provides three classes specializing in file I/O. The file stream classes are as follows:

ifstream:	Specializes in disk file input.
ofstream:	Specializes in disk file output
fstream:	Handles disk file input and output.

These classes are derived from *istream*, *ostream*, and *iostream* respectively. Therefore, they inherit all the functionality previously discussed (overloaded << & >> for built-in types, manipulators, format flags, stream states, etc).

File Stream Constructors

Each one of the File stream classes offers four constructors. The constructors enable you to do the following:

- Construct an object without opening a file:

```
ifstream();
ofstream();
fstream();
```

- Construct an object, open a specified file, and attach the object to the file:

```
ifstream(const char* name,
        int omode = ios::in,
        int prot  = filebuf::openprot);
```

```
ofstream(const char* name,
        int omode = ios::out,
        int prot  = filebuf::openprot);

fstream (const char* name,
        int omode,
        int prot= filebuf::openprot);
```

- Construct an object and attach the object to an already opened file; the file handle (descriptor) is specified:

```
ifstream(int f);
ofstream(int f);
fstream (int f);
```

- Construct an object associated with a specified buffer; the object is attached to an already opened file; the file handle (descriptor) is specified.

```
ifstream(int f, char* b, int len);
ofstream(int f, char* b, int len);
fstream (int f, char* b, int len);
```

Opening a File

You can use the *ifstream*, *ofstream*, or *fstream* constructors to open a file. The following example illustrates the *ifstream* and *ofstream* constructors:

```
////////////////////////////////////////////////////
// FILEUPPR.C: Using ifstreams and ofstreams...    //
////////////////////////////////////////////////////
#include <iostream.h>
```

```
#include <fstream.h>
#include <stdlib.h>
#include <ctype.h>


int main( void )
{
    // Prompt for input file
    cout << "Please enter an input file: ";

    // Read file name
    char fname[_MAX_PATH];
    cin  >> fname;

    // Open input file
    ifstream ifs( fname );

    // Check stream...
    if ( !ifs )
    {
        // If error, terminate...
        cout << "Unable to open file...";
        return 0;
    }

    // Prompt for output name
    cout << "Please enter an output file: ";

    // Read file name
    cin  >> fname;

    // Attempt to open output file
    ofstream ofs( fname );
```

```
// Check stream
if ( !ofs )
{
    // If error, terminate...
    cout << "Unable to open file...";
    return 0;
}

char c;

// While no error
while( ifs && ofs )
{
    // Read on character
    ifs.get( c );

    // Convert to upper case
    c = toupper( c );

    // Write to outstream
    ofs.put( c );

    // Inform user we're alive!
    cout << '.';
}

// Task accomplished...
cout << endl
    << "The output file is an upper cased "
    << "copy of the input file..."
    << endl;

return 0;
}
```

You also can use the *open* method to open a file. The following example uses the *fstream* open function:

```cpp
/////////////////////////////////////////////////////////
// OPEN.CPP: Using C++ Stream to open a file...        //
/////////////////////////////////////////////////////////
#include <iostream.h>
#include <fstream.h>
#include <stdlib.h>


int main( void )
{
    // Unopened stream object
    fstream fin;

    // Prompt for input..
    cout << "Please enter a file name: ";

    // Read file name
    char name[_MAX_PATH];
    cin  >> name;

    // Open input file..
    fin.open( name, ios::in );

    // Check stream status
    if ( fin )
    {
        // Inform user of success
        cout << "File was successfully opened. "
            << endl;

        // Close file
        fin.close();
    }
```

```
    else
    {
        // Error ...
        cout << "Unable to open file "
                << name
                << endl;
    }
    return 0;
}
```

The parameters expected by *open* have similar meaning to the one passed to the file stream constructors.

Open Modes

When opening a file, you can specify a *mode* parameter to control how the file is opened. The parameter can be formed using the following bit-mask enumerators defined in the class *ios*:

```
// stream operation mode
enum open_mode  {
    in    = 0x01,    // open for reading
    out   = 0x02,    // open for writing
    ate   = 0x04,    // seek to eof upon original open
    app   = 0x08,    // append mode: all additions at eof
    trunc    = 0x10, // truncate file if already exists
    nocreate = 0x20, // open fails if file doesn't exist
    noreplace= 0x40, // open fails if file already exists
    binary   = 0x80  // binary (not text) file
    };
```

The *mode* parameter in the constructors and *open* methods of the *ifstream* and *ofstream* classes have default values. They are *ios::in* and *ios::out*, respectively.

Using Open Modes

The following example illustrates the uses of the *mode* paremeter:

```cpp
/////////////////////////////////////////////////////////
// MODE.CPP: Using the open modes of iostream...       //
/////////////////////////////////////////////////////////
#include <iostream.h>
#include <fstream.h>

const int  MAX_LEN = 80;
const char fname[] = "NEWFILE";

int main( void )
{
    // Create new file only if it does not exist!
    ofstream ofs( fname, ios::out¦ios::noreplace );

    // Check stream status
    if ( !ofs )
    {
        // Report error and terminate
        cout << "Error! " << fname
            << "already exists."
            << endl;

        return  0;
    }
    else
```

```
{
    // Write a line to new file
    ofs  << "Hello, I am a new file...";

    // Close new file
    ofs.close();

    // Declare a new stream object
    fstream fs;

    // Open file and seek to EOF
    fs.open( fname, ios::out¦ios::ate );

    // Append a message...
    fs   << "who's been appended to!";

    // Close file
    fs.close();

    // Reopen file for input
    ifstream ifs( fname );

    // Check stream status
    if ( ifs )
    {
        // Prelude to...
        cout << "And the old file said: "
             << endl;

        // an old ...
        char line[MAX_LEN];
        ifs.getline( line, sizeof(line) );

        // file's saying...
        cout  << line;
```

```
        }
        else
        {
            // Report errors
            cout << "Error reopening "
                << fname
                << endl;
        }
    }
    return 0;
}
```

Changing a Stream's Buffer

You can control the buffering of a stream via the *setbuf* method. The function associates the stream with the specified buffer:

```
void setbuf(char *p, int len);
```

p: address of buffer
len: length of buffer

Closing a File

The file stream classes provide a *close( )* method to

- Flush the stream's contents
- Close the associated file

Unformatted I/O

The IOStream library provides several functions for nontranslated I/O. These functions enable you to read and write bytes without modification and are often used when reading or writing binary files. The following section covers binary file I/O and describes the related functions provided by unformatted I/O.

Binary File I/O

In binary mode, I/O is not interpreted. Bytes are read and written without any modification. To open a file in binary mode, include the *ios::binary* flag in the *open_mode* parameter passed to the file stream constructor or to the open function. The following sample opens a file in text and binary mode:

```
///////////////////////////////////////////////////
// BIN_TXT.CPP: Opening in binary vs. text mode...  //
///////////////////////////////////////////////////

#include <iostream.h>
#include <fstream.h>
#include <stdlib.h>
```

```cpp
int main( void )
{
    cout << "Please enter input file name: ";

    char name[_MAX_PATH];
    cin  >> name;

    ifstream ifbin( name, ios::in¦ios::binary );

    ifstream iftxt( name, ios::in );

    if ( !iftxt ¦¦ !ifbin )
    {
        cout << "Error opening file "
            << name
            << endl;

        return 0;
    }

    int countInBin = 0;
    do
    {
        if ( ifbin.get() != EOF )
            countInBin++;
    } while( ifbin );

    cout << "Num. of chars read in binary    = "
        << countInBin
        << endl;

    int countInTxt = 0;
    do
    {
```

```
        if ( iftxt.get() != EOF )
            countInTxt++;
    } while( iftxt );

    cout << "Num. of chars read in text mode = "
         << countInTxt
         << endl;

    return 0;
}
```

Text Mode versus Binary Mode

When you open a file in text mode (i.e. do not specify ios::binary),
the following things happen:

- Every carriage return/line feed combination read is
  converted to a single line feed.

- Every line feed written to the stream is converted into
  a carriage return/line feed pair.

See the BIN_TXT.CPP sample.

Reading Raw Data

The *read* function enables you to extract up to a specified number of
characters from a stream into buffer:

```
istream& istream::read(          char* p, int len);
istream& istream::read(   signed char* p, int len);
istream& istream::read(unsigned char* p, int len);
```

p:	Buffer in which to store characters read
len:	Maximum number of characters to read

Writing Raw Data

The *write* function enables you to insert a specified number of characters from a buffer into a stream.

```
ostream& ostream::write(const          char* s, int n);
ostream& ostream::write(const   signed char* s, int n);
ostream& ostream::write(const unsigned char* s, int n);
```

s:	Source buffer
n:	Number of characters to write

The following example illustrates the use of the *read* and *write* methods in binary operations:

```
/////////////////////////////////////////////////////
// BIN_IO.CPP: Constrasts binary and text I/O...    //
/////////////////////////////////////////////////////
#include <iostream.h>
#include <fstream.h>

int    i  = 12345;
long   l  = 98765432;
float  f  = 4.536271;
double d  = 2.4e12;
char msg[]= "Hello";


const char bFname[] = "_IO.BIN";
const char tFname[] = "_IO.TXT";
```

```cpp
int main( void )
{
    // -------------------------------------- //
    // First perform operations in text mode    //
    // ...................................... //
    ofstream ofs( tFname );
    if ( ofs )
    {
        ofs << i  << '\t'
            << l  << '\t'
            << f  << '\t'
            << d  << '\t'
            << msg
            << endl;

        ofs.close();
    }

    ifstream ifs( tFname );
    if ( ifs )
    {
        ifs >> i
            >> l
            >> f
            >> d
            >> msg;

        ifs.close();
    }

    // ---------------------- //
    // Now use binary mode... //
    // ...................... //
```

```
ofs.open( bFname, ios::out¦ios::binary );
if ( ofs )
{
    ofs.write( (char*)&i, sizeof(i) );
    ofs.write( (char*)&l, sizeof(l) );
    ofs.write( (char*)&f, sizeof(f) );
    ofs.write( (char*)&d, sizeof(d) );
    ofs.write(msg, sizeof(msg));

    ofs.close();
}

ifs.open( bFname, ios::in¦ios::binary );
if ( ifs )
{
    ifs.read( (char*)&i, sizeof(i) );
    ifs.read( (char*)&l, sizeof(l) );
    ifs.read( (char*)&f, sizeof(f) );
    ifs.read( (char*)&d, sizeof(d) );
    ifs.read(msg, sizeof(msg));
}

    return 0;
}
```

Reading a Character

The method *int istream::get()* can be used to extract a single character from a stream. The following example illustrates:

```
///////////////////////////////////////////////////////
// GET1.CPP: Using 'int get()' to read a character.. //
///////////////////////////////////////////////////////
```

```cpp
#include <iostream.h>


int main( void )
{
    int ch;

    cout << "Enter a number followed by #: ";

    while( ( ch = cin.get() ) != '#' )
    {
        if ( ch == EOF )
            break;

        cout << (char)ch;
    }
    return 0;
}
```

You also can use one of the following overloaded versions of the *get* function to read a character from a stream:

> *istream&*   *istream::get(char&);*
>
> *istream&*   *istream::get(signed char&);*
>
> *istream&*   *istream::get(unsigned char&);*

The following example illustrates:

```cpp
////////////////////////////////////////////////////
// GET2.CPP: Using 'int get(char&)'                //
////////////////////////////////////////////////////

#include <iostream.h>
```

```
int main( void )
{
    char ch;

    cout << "Enter a number followed by #: ";

    while( cin.get( ch ) )  // Calls operator void*();
    {
        if ( ch == '#' )
            break;

        cout << (char)ch;
    }
    return 0;
}
```

Reading a String

The C++ library offers the *get* and *getline* function for retrieving characters up to a delimiter. They are often used when reading strings.

get

The method *istream& istream::get(char* _p, int _l, char _t)* can be used to extract characters from a stream until

- The delimiter *_t* (defaults to line feed, \n) is found.

- *_l* number of characters have been fetched.

- end-of-File is reached.

The following example illustrates the *get* function:

```
///////////////////////////////////////////////////
// GET3.CPP: Using 'int get(char*, int, int);       //
///////////////////////////////////////////////////

#include <iostream.h>
#include <limits.h>

const int MAX_LEN = 0x50;

int main( void )
{
    char fname[MAX_LEN];
    char lname[MAX_LEN];

    // Prompt for first name
    cout << "Enter your first name :";

    // Read name using get()
    cin.get( fname, sizeof( fname ) );

    // Display greeting...
    cout << "Hello " << fname << endl;

    // Prompt for last name
    cout << "Enter your last name :";

    // Clear input: delimiter was not extracted!!
    cin.ignore( INT_MAX, '\n' );
```

```
    // Read name using get()
    cin.get( lname, sizeof( lname ) );

    // Display greeting...
    cout << "Hello " << fname << ' '
         << lname    << '!'    << endl;

    return 0;
}
```

getline

The following method can be used to extract characters from a stream until the delimiter _t (defaults to line feed, \n) is found, until _l-1 number of characters have been fetched, or until *end-of-File* is reached:

```
istream istream::getline(char *_p, int _l, char_t)
```

Note: The *getline* function extracts the delimiter, but it is not stored in the buffer.

The following example illustrates the *getline* function:

```
//////////////////////////////////////////////////////////
// GETLINE.CPP: Using getline for input...              //
//////////////////////////////////////////////////////////
#include <iostream.h>

const int MAX_LEN = 0x50;

int main( void )
{
```

```
      char fname[MAX_LEN];
      char lname[MAX_LEN];

      // Prompt for first name
      cout << "Enter your first name :";

      // Read first name
      cin.getline( fname, sizeof( fname ) );

      // Prompt for last name
      cout << "Enter your last name :";

      // Read last name
      cin.getline( lname, sizeof( lname ) );

      // Display greeting...
      cout << "Hello " << fname << ' '
           << lname    << '!'   << endl;

      return 0;
}
```

Commonly Used Stream Functions

Besides the overloaded *insertion* and *extraction* operators and unformatted I/O routines mentioned previously, the C++ stream library offers a vast array of functions. The following section describes the commonly used ones.

Skipping Characters on Input

To skip characters on input, you can use the following method:

```
istream& istream::ignore(int n=1, int d=EOF)
```

This function extracts up to *n* number of characters (defaults to 1) unless the delimiter *d* (defaults to EOF) is encountered. The delimiter is extracted from the stream.

Requesting an Extraction Count

The *gcount* function, *int istream::gcount();*, returns the number of characters extracted by the last unformatted input function. This number can be reset because some routines involved with formatted input call unformatted input functions.

Peeking at the Next Character

The *peek* function returns the next character without extracting it from an input stream:

```
int istream::peek();
```

The function returns EOF if the stream's status flag is nonzero.

Putting Back an Extracted Character

The *putback* function puts back the last character extracted from an input stream.

```
istream& istream::putback( char ch );
```

Seeking within a Stream

The *seekg* and *seekp* functions can be used to set the pointer of an input and output stream, respectively:

```
istream& istream::seekg(streampos);
istream& istream::seekg(streamoff, ios:::seek_dir);

ostream& ostream::seekp(streampos);
ostream& ostream::seekp(streamoff, ios::seek_dir);
```

Telling a Stream's Position

The *tellg* and *tellp* functions can be used to find the current position of an input stream and output stream, respectively.

```
streampos istream::tellg();
streampos ostream::tellp();
```

InCore Formatting

The C++ stream library supports input and output operations on memory via the *istrstream* and *ostrstream* classes. A third class, *strstream*, supports both types of operations.

istrstream

istrstream provides an interface for formatted in-memory extractions. You can create an istrstream object by passing a buffer and an optional size. The size is not required if the buffer is null terminated. The following example illustrates:

```
/////////////////////////////////////////////////////
// ISTRSTRM.CPP: Using an istrstream...              //
/////////////////////////////////////////////////////
#include <strstrea.h>

int main( void )
{
    char info[] = "Symphonies 9 "
                  "PianoConcertos  5";

    istrstream stat( info );

    char musicType[20];
    int  number;

    for( int i=0; i<2; i++ )
    {
        stat >> musicType;
        stat >> number;
```

```
        cout << "L. Beethoven wrote "
             << number  << '\t'
             << musicType
             << endl;
    }


    return 0;
}
```

ostrstream

ostrstream provides an interface for formatted in-memory insertions.
You can create an ostrstream by providing a character buffer and a size.
The ostrstream class also contains a default constructor that allocates a
buffer and dynamically resizes the latter at runtime if necessary. The
following example illustrates the two constructors:

```
///////////////////////////////////////////////////
// OSTRSTR1.CPP: Creating ostrstreams...          //
///////////////////////////////////////////////////

#include <strstrea.h>

int main( void )
{
    //
    // Create ostrstream with
    // dynamic/resizable buffer...
    //
    ostrstream  osstr_a;
```

```
    char    buffer[100];
   //
    // Create ostrstream with
    // supplied buffer...
   //
    ostrstream   osstr_b( buffer, sizeof(buffer) );

   // ...

    return 0;
}
```

Besides constructors and destructors, ostrstream provides two useful methods:

- *char* ostrstream::str()*: This method returns a pointer to the buffer of the ostrstream. This method also freezes the array. When using ostrstreams with dynamic objects, calling *str()* transfers ownership of the dynamic buffer to you. You subsequently must delete the buffer or return ownership of the buffer to the ostrstream by calling:

   ```
   oss->rdbuf()->freeze(0);
   ```

- *int ostrstream::pcount()*: This method returns the number of bytes that have been stored into the buffer.

The following example illustrates the use of an ostrstream with a dynamic buffer:

```
///////////////////////////////////////////////////////
// OSTRSTR2.CPP: Using ostrstrem with dynamic buffer //
///////////////////////////////////////////////////////

#include <strstrea.h>
```

```
int main( void )
{
    //
    // Create ostrstream with
    // dynamic/resizable buffer...
    //
    ostrstream  oss;

    int i = 10;
    char *str = "The value is ";

    //
    // Format ostrstream by misc. insertions
    //
    oss  << str
         << i
         << ends;

    //
    // Display results of insertion
    // by using str() method
    //
    cout << oss.str();


    //
    // Transfer ownership of dynamic buffer
    // back to ostrstream object for proper
    // cleanup.
    //
    oss.rdbuf()->freeze(0);

    return 0;
}
```

ostrstreams Are Not Automatically Null-Terminated

After performing operations on an ostrstream, you must explicitly append a null charater to the stream. Otherwise, the *str( )* method will probably return a pointer to a non null-terminated string.

Using Append Mode To Concatenate Strings

You can create an ostrstream in append mode by setting *ios::ate* or *ios::app* in the optional third parameter to the constructor. This enables you to pass a null terminated string as buffer and insertion will begin at the null character:

```
////////////////////////////////////////////////////////////
// OSS_CAT.CPP: Using ostrstream in append mode...   //
////////////////////////////////////////////////////////////

#include <strstrea.h>
#include <time.h>

int main( void )
{
    char msg[100] = "Now is: ";

    char  buffer[100];
    //
    // Create ostrstream with supplied buffer.
    // Open in append mode; insertions will
    // being at the null character...
    //
    ostrstream  oss( msg, sizeof(msg), ios::out¦ios::app );
```

```
        time_t t_var;
        time( &t_var );

        oss  << ctime( &t_var )
             << ends;

        cout << oss.str()
             << endl;

        return 0;
}
```

Summary

The C++ streams library offers a simple and consistent interface with a powerful and extensible implementation. Included are classes to perform input and output operations on the standard devices, disk files and character arrays. They all inherit the functionality found in the core objects of the hierarchy and can be manipulated in a uniform manner. Borland C++ provides the *constream* class that illustrates how to extend the standard library. If you are adventurous, you may consider browsing through *constrea.h* to examine how you can enhance the IOStream library with classes of your own.

Chapter 8
C++ Templates

C++ *templates* allow you to provide generic definitions for classes or functions in terms of arbitrary types. These definitions can then be used by the compiler to generate classes or functions for specific data types. As a result, templates offer an efficient way to implement routines commonly written many times for different data types. They are also used extensively for container classes. This chapter covers the syntax and use of templates and provides illustrating examples. The template-related compiler settings are also discussed.

Parametized Types

C++ templates often are referred to as Parametized Types. They allow you to have the compiler generate new classes or functions by specifying types as parameters.

Function Templates

A *function template* provides a generic definition from which the compiler may automatically generate or instantiate a function.

Function Template: Syntax

The syntax for a function template is:

```
template <tmpl_arg_list>
ret_type funcName( args ... )
{
      // function body
}
```

The keyword template is followed by one or more arguments enclosed within less-than < and greater-than > brackets and separated by commas. Each argument consists of the keyword *class* followed by an identifier representing a type. Then the function definition follows. It is similar to a non-template function definition except that one or more arguments use the types specified in the template argument list.

Defining Function Templates

The following example illustrates a few function template definitions:

```cpp
/////////////////////////////////////////////////////
// FUNCTMPL.CPP: Sample function templates...        //
/////////////////////////////////////////////////////


//
// Function template 'func': takes one parameter of
//                           arbitrary type...
//
template <class T>
void func( T t )
{
    // function body
}


//
// Function template 'Swap': takes an array of arbitrary
//                           type and two integers..
//                           Swaps the contents of the
//                           array at the specified
//                           indices
//
template <class T>
void Swap( T t[], int indx1, int indx2 )
{
    T tmp     = t[indx1];
    t[indx1] = t[indx2];
    t[indx2] = tmp;
}
```

```
//
// Function Template 'func_1': expects two parameters
//                             of the same type...
//
template <class T>
void func_1( T t1, T t2 )
{
    // function body
}


//
  // Function Template 'func_2': expects two parameters
  //                             of different (or
//                               same) type.
//
template <class T1, class T2>
void func_2( T1 t1, T2 t2 )
{
    // function body
}
```

It is common to sort the members of an array. You can use a function template to provide a generic definition for sorting arrays of any types. The following example illustrates a possible implementation of the function template using the Bubble Sort algorithm:

```
///////////////////////////////////////////////////////
// SORTTMPL.H: Template function for sorting arrays. //
///////////////////////////////////////////////////////

#if !defined(__SORTTMPL_H)
#define        __SORTTMPL_H


//
// Function Template for generic sorting of arrays.
// ** NOTE: When sorting arrays of user-defined types,
//          the type must overload the '>' operator.
//
template <class T>  void  sort( T array[], size_t size )
{
    for ( int i=0; i<size-i; i++ )
        for( int j=size-1; i<j; j-- )
            if ( array[j-1] > array[j] )
            {
                T tmp      = array[j];
                array[j]   = array[j-1];
                array[j-1] = tmp;
            }
}


#endif  //   __SORTTMPL_H
```

Using Function Templates

After declaring a function template, you can merely call the function: the compiler will automatically instantiate a function body for the types you specified. For example, to use the *sort* function template defined above, you can merely call the function with an array and a size parameter. The following example illustrates this:

```
//////////////////////////////////////////////////////
// SORT1.CPP: Using the sort function template...    //
//////////////////////////////////////////////////////

#include <iostream.h>
#include "sorttmpl.h"          // Function Template 'sort'


int main( void )
{
    //
    // Create array if integers
```

```
    //
    int iarray[] = { 30, 27, 45, 10, 23, 7, 4, 89 };

    //
    // Sort array: compiler automatically instantiate
    //              a template function:
    //                      void sort( int[], size_t );
    //
    sort( iarray, sizeof( iarray )/sizeof( iarray[0] ) );

    //
    // Display contents of sorted array
    //
    for ( int i=0;
          i< sizeof( iarray )/sizeof( iarray[0] );
          i++ )
        cout << "iarray[" << i << "] = " << iarray[i]
                                      << endl;

    return 0;
}
```

The sort template also can be used for user-defined classes provided that the class overloads the > operator used for comparison in the sort function template. The following example illustrates the sort template with a user-defined type:

```
///////////////////////////////////////////////////////
// SORT2.CPP: Using the sort function template...    //
///////////////////////////////////////////////////////

#include <iostream.h>
#include "sorttmpl.h"        // Function Template 'sort'

//
// class Amount: encapsulates a dollar/cents value
```

```
//
class Amount
{
        long dollars;
        int  cents;

    public:
        Amount( long _d, int _c )
        {
            dollars = _d;
            cents   = _c;
        }

        //
        // Overloaded '>' operator to allow comparison
        // of instances of amount...
        //
        int operator > ( const Amount& ) const;

        //
        // Friend function to allow access to private
        // data members when formatting output
        //
        friend ostream& operator << ( ostream&, Amount& );
};


int Amount::operator > ( const Amount& _amt ) const
{
    return ( dollars > _amt.dollars  ) ||
           ( dollars == _amt.dollars &&
             cents   > _amt.cents    );
}
```

```cpp
ostream& operator << ( ostream& os, Amount &_amt )
{
    os << "$" << _amt.dollars
        << '.' << _amt.cents;

    return os;
}



int main( void )
{
    //
    // Create array if integers
    //
    Amount amtArray[] = {
                            Amount( 19, 10 ),
                            Amount( 99, 99 ),
                            Amount( 99, 95 ),
                            Amount( 19, 95 )
                    };

    //
    // Sort array: compiler automatically instantiate
    //           a template function:
    //               void sort( Amount[], size_t );
    //
    sort( amtArray, sizeof( amtArray )/sizeof( amtArray[0] ) );

    //
    // Display contents of sorted array
    //
    for ( int i=0;
          i< sizeof( amtArray )/sizeof( amtArray[0] );
```

```
        i++ )
    cout << "amtArray[" << i << "] = " << amtArray[i]
                                            << endl;

    return 0;
}
```

min and max as function templates

The header file *stdlib.h* included with your copy of Borland C++ provides definitions for the function templates *min* and *max* when used in C++ mode:

```
template <class T> inline const T& min( const T& t1,
                                        const T& t2 )
{
    return t1>t2 ? t2 : t1;
}

template <class T> inline const T& max( const T& t1,
                                        const T& t2 )
{
    return t1>t2 ? t1 : t2;
}
```

The function templates allow the compiler to automatically instanti-ate versions of the *min* or *max* function whenever these functions are called with two parameters of the same type. The parameters may be a built-in type or a user-defined type with the *operator>( )* defined. The following example illustrates this:

```
////////////////////////////////////////////////////////
// MAX.CPP: Using the max() function template...      //
////////////////////////////////////////////////////////

#include <stdlib.h>
```

```
#include <iostream.h>
#include <classlib\date.h>


int main( void )
{

    int i1 = 10;
    int i2 = 20;

    //
    // The following causes the compiler to
    // instantiate and call the template function:
    //    const int& max( const int&, const int& );
    //
    cout << "Max integer is "
         << max( i1, i2 )
         << endl;



    float f1 = 3.456;
    float f2 = 3.789;

    //
    // The following causes the compiler to
    // instantiate and call the template function:
    //    const float& max( const float&, const float& );
    //
    cout << "Max float is "
         << max( f1, f2 )
         << endl;
```

continues

continued

```
    TDate d1( 8, 8, 65);
    TDate d2(10, 3, 69);

    //
      // The following causes the compiler to
      // instantiate and call the template function:
    //    const TDate& max( const TDate&, const TDate& );
    //
    TDate d3 = max( d1, d2 );

    cout << "Max date is " << d3
         <<  endl;

    return 0;
}
```

Function Templates versus Template Functions

A function template is a template definition from which the compiler can create functions. Functions created from a function template are known as template functions.

Overloading Function Templates

Just like regular functions, function templates can be overloaded. That is, you may provide more than one function template with the same name as long as they have different signatures: different parameter types or different number of arguments. This is shown in the following example:

```
/////////////////////////////////////////////////
// OVRTMPL.CPP: Overloading function templates...    //
/////////////////////////////////////////////////

#include <iostream.h>

//
//  Returns greater of two parameters
//
template <class T>
T  getMax( T t1, T t2 )
{
    return t1 > t2 ? t1 : t2;
}



//
   //  Returns value of greatest
   //  element in array
//
template <class T>
T  getMax( T t[], size_t size )
{
    T retVal = t[0];
    for( int i=0; i<size; i++ )
        if ( t[i] > retVal )
            retVal = t[i];
    return retVal;
}


int main( void )
{
    int i1 = 3;
```

```
    int i2 = 5;

    int iarray[] = { 3, 9, 5, 8 };

    cout << "max int = " << getMax( i1, i2 ) << endl;

    cout << "max int = "
         << getMax(iarray, sizeof(iarray)/sizeof(iarray[0]))
         << endl;

    return 0;
}
```

Specializing Function Templates

A *Specialized Template Function* is a regular function sharing the name of a Template function but defined for specific types. You can provide specialized template functions for data types where the generic template function is inappropriate. For example, the *getMax* template function defined above should not be used for strings (char*, char[]) since the function generated by the compiler will merely compare memory locations. The following example provides a specialized function for that purpose:

```
////////////////////////////////////////////////////////
// OVRTMPL.CPP: Overloading function templates...    //
////////////////////////////////////////////////////////

#include <iostream.h>
#include <string.h>

//
//  Returns greater of two parameters
```

```cpp
//
template <class T>
T  getMax( T t1, T t2 )
  {
      return t1 > t2 ? t1 : t2;
}


//
// Specialized version of getMax to handle
// strings ( char*, char[] );
//
char* getMax( char* s1, char* s2 )
{
    return strcmp( s1, s2 ) > 1 ? s1 : s2;
}


int main( void )
{
    int i1 = 3;
    int i2 = 5;

    cout << "max int = " << getMax( i1, i2 ) << endl;


    char *s1 = "Golden Eagle";
    char *s2 = "Perigrine Falcon";

    cout << "max str = " << getMax( s1, s2 ) << endl;

    return 0;
}
```

Resolving a Reference to a Function

When the compiler encounters a reference to a function, the following algorithm is used to find a match for the reference:

- Find a (non-template) function with matching parameters.

- If none was found, find a function template from which a template function *with an exact match* can be generated.

- If no function templates provided an exact match, then reconsider non-template functions allowing conversion of types.

Note that no conversion is performed when considering function templates.

Class Templates

A *class template* provides a generic definition for a family of classes in terms of arbitrary types or constants. The template defines the data members and member functions of the class. After defining a class template, you can instruct the compiler to generate a new class for a specific data type or constant based on the template definition.

Class Template: Syntax

The syntax for a class template is:

```
template <tmpl_arg_list>
class className
{
      // class body
}
```

The keyword template is followed by one or more arguments enclosed within less-than <and greater-than > brackets and separated by commas. Each argument is:

- either a type name followed by an identifier

- or the keyword *class* followed by an identifier representing a parametized type.

Then the class definition follows. It is similar to the definition of non-template classes except for the use of the template argument list.

Type Parameters versus Nontype Parameters

The template parameters consisting of the class keyword followed by an identifier are often referred to as type parameters. That is, they inform the compiler that the template expects a type. The template parameters consisting of a type name and an identifier are referred to a nontype parameters: they inform the compiler to expect a constant.

Defining Class Templates

The following example illustrates a few class template definitions:

```
/////////////////////////////////////////////////////
// CLSTMPL1.H: Class Template definition...         //
/////////////////////////////////////////////////////

  #if !defined(__CLSTMPL1_H)
  #define    __CLSTMPL1_H
```

```
#include <stdlib.h>

const size_t defStackSize = 10;


//
// TStack: Class Template for simple stack operations
//
template <class T>
class    TStack
{
    public:
        TStack( size_t size = defStackSize )
        {
            numItems = 0;
            items = new T[size];
        }

        ~TStack()
        {
            delete [] items;
        }

        void push( T t );
        T     pop();

    protected:
        int numItems;
        T     *items;
};
```

```
//
// push method of TStack template
//
template <class T>
void TStack<T>::push( T t )
{
    items[numItems++] = t;
}



//
// pop method of TStack template
//
template <class T>
T     TStack<T>::pop()
{
    return items[--numItems];
}



#endif  //   __CLSTMPL1_H
```

As illustrated above, the member functions of a class template can be defined within the body of the class (in other words, inline). When defined out-of-line, however, the function signature has the following format:

```
template <tmpl_arg_list>
ret_type className<tmpl_arg>::member_Function(params..)
{
        // body of function
}
```

As mentioned above, the parameters of a class template can be either a type or a constant. The following example illustrates a class template, MemBlock, taking a constant and another class template, TypeBlock, taking both a type and a constant as parameters.

```
/////////////////////////////////////////////////////
// CLSTMPL2.H: Class Template definition...         //
/////////////////////////////////////////////////////


#if !defined(__CLSTMPL2_H)
#define      __CLSTMPL2_H

//
// MemBlock: Class Template for a generic block of
//           memory. Expects constant when instantiated
//
template <int size>
class   MemBlock
{
    public:
        MemBlock()
        {
            p = new char[size];
        }
```

```cpp
    ~MemBlock()
     {
         delete [] p;
     }

     operator char* ()
     {
         return p;
     }

  protected:
      char *p
};




//
//TypeBlock: Class Template encapsulating a block of
//           memory for a particular type. Expects a
//           type and a constant when instantiated. . .
//
template <class T, int numElements>
class   TypeBlock
{
    public
        TypeBlock();
       ~TypeBlock();

        operator T* ();

    protected:
        T*  p;
};
```

```
template<class T, int numElements>
TypeBlock<T, numElements>::TypeBlock()
{
    p = new T[numElements];
}


template<class T, int numElements>
TypeBlock<T, numElements>::~TypeBlock()
{
    delete [] p;
}

template<class T, int numElements>
TypeBlock<T, numElements>::Operator T*()
{
    return p;
}

#endif // CLSTMPL2 H
```

Like classes, class templates can have static data members, static member functions, friend functions and classes. You cannot define an inner template within the body of an outer template declaration. However, you can declare an inner class which uses one or more of the template parameters.

Using Class Templates

To create an instance of a template class, you can simply use the class template name with its argument list within less-than and greater-than brackets as a type specifier, provided the argument list is modified as follows:

- each argument with the format class *identifier* (type parameter) is replaced with an actual type.

- each argument with the format *type identifier* (nontype parameter) is replaced with a constant expression.

The following illustrates several instantiations of the *TStack* class template:

```cpp
//////////////////////////////////////////////////////
// STACKTMP.CPP: Using the TStack Class Template...  //
//////////////////////////////////////////////////////

#include <cstring.h>
#include "clstmpl.h"          // TStack's Definition


TStack<int> stckInt1;         // Stack of 'int' using
                              // default argument of
                              // constructor

TStack<int> stckInt2( 40 );   // Stack of 'int' - Stack
                              // of up to 40 integers..

TStack<long>  *pstckLng;      // Pointer to stack of 'long'

TStack<double> dblStk[10];    // Array of stack of 'double'

TStack<string> strStck;       // Stack of 'string', a user-
                              // defined type;
                              // [see cstring.h]

// Pointer to member function of 'Stack of unsigned'
// expecting a long parameter and returning an int..
//
int (TStack<unsigned>::*mf)( long );
```

```
extern TStack<char*> cStck; // External Stack of character
                            // pointers..

extern TStack<char*> *pcStck;//External pointer to Stack
                             //of character pointers...


//
// Allocating memory for cpStck variable
//
   void InitcpStck()
   {
       pcStck = new TStack<char*>(20);
}
```

Once you've created an instance of a template class, the variable can be used just like a regular class. The following example illustrates how to create and use instances of template classes:

```
//////////////////////////////////////////////////////
// CLSTMPL1.CPP: Using class templates...            //
//////////////////////////////////////////////////////

#include <iostream.h>
#include "clstmpl1.h"


int main( void )
{
    TStack<int>  StackOfInt( 10 );

    StackOfInt.push( 33 );
    StackOfInt.push( 44 );
    StackOfInt.push( 55 );
```

```
    cout << "Values pushed are: "
         << StackOfInt.pop()     << ','
         << StackOfInt.pop()     << ','
         << StackOfInt.pop()     << endl;


    TStack<double>  StackOfDouble( 10 );

    StackOfDouble.push( 2.3456 );
    StackOfDouble.push( 4.8967 );
    StackOfDouble.push( -1.345 );

    cout << "Values pushed are: "
         << StackOfDouble.pop()   << ','
         << StackOfDouble.pop()   << ','
         << StackOfDouble.pop()   << endl;

    return 0;
}
```

The following example uses the *MemBlock* class template:

```
///////////////////////////////////////////////////
// CLSTMPL2.CPP: Using class templates...          //
///////////////////////////////////////////////////

#include <iostream.h>
#include <string.h>
#include "clstmpl2.h"


int main( void )
{
    MemBlock<512>   Half_K_Block;
```

```
    strcpy( Half_K_Block, "Have a nice day!" );
    cout << (char*) Half_K_Block << endl;

    MemBlock<1024>  One_K_Block;

    strcpy( One_K_Block, "Have a royal day!" );
    cout << (char*) One_K_Block << endl;

    return 0;
}
```

Use typedef for Template Classes

You can use the typedef keyword to simplify the use of template classes. See the following:

```
#include "clstmpl1.h"

TStack<long>    lstk;
TStack<long>  *plstk;
TStack<long>    alstk[10];

can be simplified to:

#include "clstmpl1.h"

typedef TStack<long> LStack;

LStack    lstk;
LStack *plstk;
LStack    alstk[10];
```

Specializing Class Templates

You can specialize a class template by providing explicit implementation of some of the methods for particular types. See the following example, a definition of the *TArray* class template.

```
/////////////////////////////////////////////////////
// ARRAY.H: Simple Array Class Template...          //
/////////////////////////////////////////////////////

#if !defined(__ARRAY_H)
#define      __ARRAY_H


#include <fstream.h>


const int defSize = 100;

//
// Generic Array Template: stores objects
//                         in an array...
//
template <class T>
class   TArray
{
    public:
        TArray( int size = defSize )
        {
            // ...
        };

        ~TArray()
        {
            // ...
        }
```

```
        void add( T item );

    protected:
        // data members ... etc
};


void TArray<char*>::add( char *str )
{
    // Specialized version of
    // add method for <char*>
}


template <class T>
void TArray<T>::add( T t )
{
    // Generic version of
    // add method for <T*>
}


#endif  //  _ _ARRAY_H
```

The above example provides a specialized version of the *add* method for
<char*> types. The following example illustrates the result of overriding
the *add* method:

```
/////////////////////////////////////////////////////
// SPC_CLS1.CPP: Using specialized template classes. //
/////////////////////////////////////////////////////

#include "array.h"
```

```
int main( void )
{
    int i1 = 10;

    TArray<int> iArray;
    iArray.add( i1 );


    char *msg = "Look at the rose hill!";

    //
    // The following instantiation uses the
    // generic version of the constructor..
    //
    TArray<char*> strArray;

    //
    // The following call to the 'add' method
    // calls the specialized version of 'add'
    // provided for arrays of <char*>
    //
    strArray.add( msg );

    return 0;
}
```

You can also provide a complete redefinition of the class template specialized to handle a particular type. When specializing a whole template class you must do the following:

- Provide the specialized template class definition after the definition of the generic template class.

- Provide the definition of all the member functions.

The following sample is a slightly modified version of the prior example: it provides a specialized version of the *TArray* class template for <string> types.

```
#include <cstring.h>
#include array.h

//
// Specialized version of TArray
  // template to handle type <string>
  //
class TArray<string>
{
    public:
        TArray( int size = defSize )
        {
            // ...
        }

        ~TArray()
        {
            // ...
        }

        void add( string str, int indx = -1 );
};


//
// Out-of-line specialized method add
//
void TArray<string>::add( string str, int indx )
{
    // ...
}
```

```cpp
int main( void )
{
    int i1 = 10;

    //
     // The following calls the generic
     // constructor of TArray
    //
     TArray<int> iList;



    //
     // The following calls the generic
     // add method of TArray
    //
     iList.add( i1 );


     string str( Morning at Rose Hill ! );

    //
     // The following calls the specialized
     // constructor of TArray<string>
    //
     TArray<string> sList;



     // The following calls the specialized
     // version of TArray<string>::add
    ///
     sList.add( str );

     return 0;
}
```

Templates and Compiler Switches

Borland C++ provides three settings that control how the compiler
generates code for instances of function templates and class templates.
Users of the IDE can access these settings from the Options menu:

- Choose the Options|Project menu selection. The Project Options
  dialog appears, as shown in figure 8.1.

- Expand the C++ Options topic and select Templates. The Template
  Settings dialog appears.

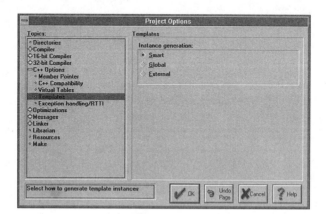

Figure 8.1. *The Project Options dialog.*

Command line users have access to the same settings with the -Jd (smart), -Jgd (global) and -Jgx (external) options.

Smart Templates

Smart template is the default compiler setting. It instructs the compiler to generate the appropriate template code for the types the template instances have been created for. This setting is appropriate for projects where a template is instantiated only after the complete template definition (the body of function templates, body of member functions, and definition of static data members) has been seen by the compiler.

Although the compiler may generate multiple definitions of the same template/type combination if the latter is used in more than one module, the linker inserts only one copy of the code for any particular instantiation in the final executable (.EXE) or dynamic library (.DLL).

> ### Insert Your Template Definition in a Header File
>
> Use a header file for your function template or class template definitions. The file should contain:
>
> - the body of function templates.
> - the body of class template member functions.
> - the definition of class template static data members.
>
> Use the *smart template* compiler option and simply include the header file in modules creating instances of the template(s).

Global and External Templates

A combination of the *Global* and *external* template settings is necessary if you create or use instances of a template before the whole template definition has been seen by the compiler. You also need to use these settings if you want the compiler to generate code for a particular template instance without creating an instance of the template. For example, a library vendor providing templates may wish to build a dynamic library with common template instantiations without actually creating template instances.

To properly use the *global* and *external* template settings you must make sure of the following::

- For any particular template/type combination, only one instantiating module has the *global* template switch enabled.

- All other modules instantiating that particular template/type combination use the *external* template settings.

In the following examples, the first module uses global template settings and instantiates a C<int> while the second module uses external settings:

```
//////////////////////////////////////////////////////
// TMPLOPT1.CPP:Using global/extern template settings//
//////////////////////////////////////////////////////

//
// The following option informs the compiler to
// generate global definitions for the template
// instances created in this module...
//
#pragma option -Jgd     // <<<<<<<<<<<<<<<<<<
```

```
//
// Class Template C
//
template<class T>
class C
{
    public:
        C();
};


//
// Constructor of C.
//
template <class T>
C<T>::C()
{
    // body of constructor
}


C<int>  CofInt;      // Causes global generation of C<int>




///////////////////////////////////////////////////////
// TMPLOPT2.CPP:Using global/extern template settings//
///////////////////////////////////////////////////////


//
// The following option informs the compiler to
// generate external references for the template
// instances created in this module. This is necessary
// since the compiler does not have access to the
// body of C<T>::C() while compiling this module...
//
#pragma option -Jgx
```

```
//
// Class Template C
//
template<class T>
class C
{
    public:
        C();
};


int main( void )
{
    C<int>  iC;            // Create External references!!

    return 0;
}
```

Drawbacks of Templates

Templates offer several advantages to the C++ programmer, including code reusability and low code maintenance. These techniques are generally very efficient compared to others used to handle different data types (such as polymorphism). Templates are also type-safe compared to preprocessor macros. You should, however, watch out for a few drawbacks:

- Your program will contain a complete set of code for every template type instantiation. This may quickly increase the size of your executable.

- Often the implementation of a template will perform well for some types but be less than optimal with other types. For example the *min* and *max* function template defined in the STDLIB.H header file.

```
template <class T> inline const T& min( const T& t1,
                                        const T& t2 )
{
    return t1>t2 ? t2 : t1;
}

template <class T> inline const T& max( const T& t1,
                                        const T& t2 )
{
    return t1>t2 ? t1 : t2;
}
```

The *min* and *max* functions are not very optimal for built in types: the use of references causes the compiler to generate additional indirection code. However, the template is suitable for large objects for which copy operations are costly so it may be useful to take advantage of *specialization* to enhance performance.

Summary

In this chapter you've seen the power and advantages of templates. Several large libraries (such as the Borland C++ Container Class Libraries) use templates extensively. You can easily create new classes and functions by instantiating the prewritten templates. Alternatively, you can opt to start building your own templates to define operations, algorithms, and functions you use during an application's development.

Chapter 9
Exception Handling

Exception handling is a standard interface for detecting and reporting unusual, unexpected, and exceptional conditions or events. It provides a formal way to divert the flow of control of a function to an unspecified section of code willing to handle the exception. Borland C++ supports two flavors of exception handling:

- C++ exception handling
- C structured exception handling

This chapter examines the syntax and usage of both mechanisms and highlights the various advantages of exception handling over the traditional methods of reporting error conditions:

- A consistent style, which in turn enhances code readability and maintenance

- The elimination of global variables and user-defined callbacks commonly used for similar purposes

- Better debugging support. The mechanism is an integral part of the language and requires support from the runtime library—the debugger offers special support to allow you to monitor exceptions

- The inability for programs to ignore errors and keep running hoping for the best

Using Exceptions and the Stack

When a function throws (C++ EH) or raises (Structured EH), an exception to halt current processing, control is transferred to a section of code whose function is still on the *call stack*. In other words, control can be transferred only to a function executed earlier and not yet terminated.

The stack is an area of memory where local (temporary) variables and the return addresses of functions are stored. On INTEL based computers, one of the registers, SP (Stack Pointer), points to the last value (word) pushed on the stack. For example, in the following sample at the label (1) within function main( ) the stack can be represented as shown in figure 9.1.

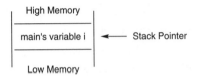

Figure 9.1. *A stack representation.*

```
/////////////////////////////////////////////////
// STACK.CPP: Understanding the call stack...      //
/////////////////////////////////////////////////
#include <fstream.h>

void func2()
{
    int l = 0x1000L;

    // (3) When control reaches this location
    //      the stack pointer points to
    //      the variable 'l'; walking up the
    //      stack (low mem -> high mem) we find:
    //         - func2's stack frame
    //         - the return address of func1()
    //         - func1's  variable 'ifs'.
    //         - func1's stack frame
    //         - the return address of main()
    //         - main's  variable 'i'.
}

void func1()
{
    ifstream ifs( "STACK.CPP" );
```

```
        // (2) Walking up the stack when
        //     control reaches this location
        //     you'll find the following:
        //         - the 'ifs' local variable
        //         - func1's stack frame
        //         - the return address of main()
        //         - main's  variable 'i'.

        func2();
}


int main( void )
{
    int    i = 0x1;

    // (1) When the instruction pointer reaches
    //     this location, the stack pointer points
    //     to the variable i, the last value
    //     'pushed' on the stack...

    func1();

    return i;
}
```

At the label (3) within function func2( ), the stack looks like figure 9.2.

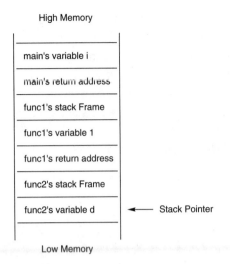

High Memory

| main's variable i |
| main's return address |
| func1's stack Frame |
| func1's variable 1 |
| func1's return address |
| func2's stack Frame |
| func2's variable d | ◄─── Stack Pointer |

Low Memory

Figure 9.2. *The stack at label (3) within func2( ).*

The term *call stack* refers to the sequence of functions called (but
not yet concluded) to reach a particular location in a program.
Figure 9.3 shows a call stack from within func2( ).

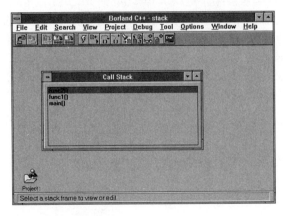

Figure 9.3. *A sample call stack.*

Stack unwinding refers to the process of popping items off the stack to destroy local variables and return control to a caller. The stack is naturally unwound when a function returns to its caller. However, the stack can also be unwound via exception handling, the longjmp( ) RTL function or by direct modification of the CPU registers. In the case of C++ exception handling, *stack unwinding* also refers to executing the destructors of local objects while popping them off the stack.

Working with C++ Exception Handling

C++ exception handling is part of the C++ ANSI specifications. The standard supports the *termination* model: that is, after an exception has been reported, it is not possible for the handler to request that control resumes at the location of the exception. C++ exceptions also do not handle asynchronous events such as hardware exceptions or interrupt service routines. Only exceptions explicitly flagged by a function are handled.

Three C++ keywords are used in the context of C++ exception handling: *try, catch,* and *throw.*

Using *try*

The *try* keyword identifies a block of code that may generate an exception. The block of code is surrounded by braces:

```
try
{
    cout << "In try-block... "
        << endl;

    func(); // func() may generate exception
}
```

The statements within the braces are said to be in a *try-block*. The body of each function called from the *try-block* is also in the *try-block*. In other words, all functions called directly or indirectly from a *try-block* are within the *try-block*.

Using *Catch*

The *catch* keyword follows a *try-block* and identifies a section of code in which control can be transferred if an exception occurs. The *catch* keyword is followed by an *exception declaration* that consists of a type name and an optional variable name in parentheses. The type name identifies the type of exception the code can handle. You can consider the *exception declaration* as a function parameter.

The block of code handling exceptions is within braces and is referred to as a *catch-handler* or as an *exception-handler*. There may be more than one *catch* statement following a *try-block*. The following example shows the *catch* statement:

```
///////////////////////////////////////////////////
// CATCH.CPP: The catch statement...              //
///////////////////////////////////////////////////
#include <iostream.h>
```

```cpp
void func( void );  // Prototype external function!

int main( void )
{
    try
    {
        cout << "In try-block... "
             << endl;

        func(); // func() may generate exception
    }

    // Handles exceptions of type 'int'
    catch( int i )
    {
    }

    // Handles exceptions of type 'const char*'
    catch( const char*  )
    {
    }

    // Handles all (unhandled) exceptions
    catch( ... )
    {
    }

    return 0;
}
```

The *catch* statement with ellipsis (...) catches exceptions of any type and must be the last *catch* statement following a *try-block*.

Using *throw*

The *throw* keyword throws an exception and causes control to be transferred to a handler. The *throw* keyword may or may not be followed by an expression.

throw with Operand

The expression following the *throw* keyword evaluates to a variable of a particular type. You can consider the operand of the *throw* keyword as the argument of a function call. The type of the operand determines which handler can catch the exception. The location of the *throw* is commonly referred to as the *throw-point*. See the following example:

```
//////////////////////////////////////////////////
// THROW.CPP: Using the throw keyword...          //
//////////////////////////////////////////////////
#include <cstring.h>

void func1()
{
    //
    // Throwing a 'const char*'
    //
    if ( something_wrong_happens )
        throw "Error encountered..";
}


void func2()
{
    //
    // Throwing a 'string' object
    //
```

```
if ( something_wrong_happens )
{
    string str( "Oops... " );
    throw  str;
}
}
```

throw with No Operand

If a *throw* expression has no operand, the exception currently being
handled is rethrown. The *throw* with no operand, therefore, can be used
only from a *catch* handler or a function directly or indirectly called from
a *catch* handler.

Catching a *throw*

When a *throw* expression is executed, the C++ runtime functions

- Make a copy of the object/variable thrown

- Unwind the stack calling the destructors of local objects going out
  of scope

- Transfer control to the nearest *catch* handler expecting a variable
  whose type is compatible with the type of the object thrown. The
  copy of the object thrown is passed as a parameter to the *catch*
  handler

The following example shows the order of events:

```
///////////////////////////////////////////////////
// XCPT1.CPP: Matching throw and catch statements... //
///////////////////////////////////////////////////
#include <fstream.h>


//
// TaleTellingClass: Simple class which informs us
//                   of its creation and destruction..
//
class TaleTellingClass
{
    public:
        TaleTellingClass()
        {
            cout << "TaleTellingClass: "
                    "Once upon a time ...."
                 << endl;
        }

        ~TaleTellingClass()
        {
            cout << "TaleTellingClass: "
                    "happily ever after... "
                 << endl;
        }
};


void function1( void )
{
    ifstream ifs( "\\INVALID\\FILE\\NAME" );

    if ( !ifs )
    {
```

```
        cout << "Throwing exception.."
            << endl;

        //
        // throwing a 'const char*'
        //
        throw "Error opening file...";
    }

    //
    // Else, file was successfully opened
    //
}


void function2( void )
{
    //
    // Create a local object to verify local
    // destructor cleanup on stack unwinding.
    //
    TaleTellingClass tellme;

    //
    // Call function which throws exception
    //
    function1();
}


int main( void )
{
    try
    {
        cout << "Entering try-block..."
```

```
            << endl;

        function2();

        cout << "Exiting  try-block..."
            << endl;
    }

    catch( int i )
    {
        cout << "int handler called with "
            << i
            << endl;

        return -1;
    }

    catch( const char* p )
    {
        cout << "char* handler called with msg "
            << '[' <<  p  << ']'
            << endl;

        return -1;
    }

    catch( ... )
    {
        cout << "catch_all handler... "
            << endl;
        return -1;
    }

    return 0;   // Safe trip!!
}
```

The output from the above sample is shown below:

```
Entering try-block...
TaleTellingClass: Once upon a time ....
Throwing exception..
TaleTellingClass: happily ever after...
char* handler called with msg [Error opening file...]
```

In the preceding example note that

- The destructor of the local variable *tellme* from *function2* was properly called although controlled was transferred from *function1* directly to the handler in *main*.

- The *Exiting try-block* message in function *main* was never executed.

- The second handler was called for this exception because its parameter type matched the type of the object thrown (i.e. const char*).

Exception Type and Copy Constructors

An error is generated if the copy constructor of the object thrown is not accessible at the throw point. For example, you may not throw a type or a pointer type with a non-public copy constructor, unless you are a *friend*. See the following example:

```
/////////////////////////////////////////////////////////
// NOTHROW.CPP: Exceptions and access...                //
/////////////////////////////////////////////////////////

//
// Class with non-public copy constructor
//
class TCopCon
{
```

```
    public:
        TCopCon();

    protected:
        TCopCon( const TCopCon& );

    friend void funcB( void );
};


void funcA( void )
{
    if ( step_one_goes_wrong )
    {
        TCopCon np;

        // The following throw expression
        // generates the following msg:
        //
        // Error nothrow.cpp 45:
        //     'TCopCon::TCopCon(const TCopCon &)'
        //     is not accessible in function funcA()

        throw np;
    }

    // ...
}


void funcB( void )
{
    if ( step_one_goes_wrong )
    {
        TCopCon np;
```

continues

continued

```
      //
      // The following is OK
      //
      throw np;
  }

  // ...
}
```

Matching Exception Types

As shown by the exception handling syntax and the preceding example, an exception is both a variable and a data type. You may also say that an exception is both an object and a class:

> You *throw* a variable and *catch* a type.

> You *throw* an object and *catch* a class.

After an exception is thrown, the C++ runtime routines look for an appropriate handler. A matching handler is found if

- The type of the object thrown is the same as the type expected by the handler. In other words, if a *T* is thrown, a handler catching a *T*, *const T*, *T&*, or *const T&* constitutes a match.

- The type of the handler is a public base class of the object thrown.

- The handler expects a pointer, and the object thrown is a pointer that can be converted to the handler's pointer type via standard pointer conversion.

Carefully Ordering Catch Handlers

You must be careful when ordering your catch handlers. A handler expecting a base class automatically hides a handler expecting a class derived from the base. Similarly, a handler expecting a void pointer automatically hides any following handler expecting a pointer type. See the following example:

```cpp
/////////////////////////////////////////////////////////
// CATCHORD.CPP: Order of catch handlers...            //
/////////////////////////////////////////////////////////
#include <iostream.h>

class Base
{
};

class Derived : public Base
{
};

void funcA()
{
    Derived d;
    throw    d;
}

void funcB()
{
    throw "Error in funcA()";
}


int main( void )
{
```

continues

continued

```
try
{
    funcA();
}

//
// The following catch handlers are incorrectly
// placed: The 'derived&' handler should precede
// the base handler. With the current order,
// the 'derived&' handler will never handle
// an exception !!
//
catch( Base& )
{   cout << "Caught Base&" << endl;  }

catch( Derived& )
{   cout << "Caught Derived&" << endl;  }


try
{
    funcB();
}

//
// The following catch handlers are incorrectly
// placed: The 'const char*' handler should precede
// the 'void*' handler. With the current order,
// the 'const char*' handler will never handle
// an exception !!
//
catch( void* )
{   cout << "Caught void*" << endl;  }
```

```
    catch( const char* )
    {   cout << "Caught const char*" << endl;  }

    return 0;
}
```

When run, the preceding program displays:

```
Caught Base&
Caught void*
```

Using *terminate()* and Unhandled Exceptions

If no matching handler is found for an exception thrown, the *terminate( )* function is called. The *terminate( )* function calls the *abort( )* function, which abnormally terminates the current process.

You can install your own termination function by using the *set_terminate* function defined in *EXCEPT.H*:

```
typedef void (_RTLENTRY *terminate_function)();
// ...
terminate_function _RTLENTRY set_terminate(terminate_function);
```

The function returns the address of the previous termination function. Your termination routine must not return to its caller nor throw an exception.

The termination function is also called if an exception is thrown during the execution of a destructor—if the destructor was called as a result of stack unwinding caused by a prior exception.

Working with Exception Specifications

You can specify a list of exceptions that a function can directly or indirectly throw by following the function declarator with an *exception specification*. The *exception specification* has the following format:

throw (type, type, ...)

An *exception specification* with no *types* implies that the function should not throw any exceptions. Functions with no *exception specification* can throw any type of exception. The following example shows *exception specifications:*

```
//////////////////////////////////////////////////////
// XCPTSPEC.CPP: Using Exception Specifications...   //
//////////////////////////////////////////////////////


struct xClass
{
    int i;
};


void funcA( void ) throw( int )
{
    // Function should only throw int exception
}


void funcB( void ) throw( long, xClass* )
{
    // Function should only throw longs,
    // xClass pointers or pointers to classes
    // derived from xClass
}
```

```
void funcC( void ) throw()
{
    // Function should not throw any exceptions
}
```

Working with Unexpected Exceptions

The *exception list* is not enforced by the compiler. That is, a function can directly or indirectly throw an exception it promised not to. For example, the following will compile without an error or warning:

```
void func( void ) throw ( int )
{
    throw "Oops...!";
}
```

Violation of the *exception list* is only detected at runtime. Unanticipated exceptions cause the *unexpected( )* function to be called. By default, the *unexpected* function simply calls the *terminate( )* function. However, you can use the *set_unexpected* function to have your own routine called when a function throws an exception not listed in its *exception list*. The *set_unexpected* function is defined in the *EXCEPT.H* header file:

```
typedef void (_RTLENTRY *unexpected_function)();
// ...
unexpected_function _RTLENTRY
set_unexpected(unexpected_function);
```

The function returns the address of the previous unexpected function. Your unexpected routine may not return to its caller. However, the routine may throw an exception.

Working with Constructors and Exceptions

The following section describes the scenario in cases in which an exception is directly or indirectly thrown from the constructor of a class.

Local Objects

Only fully constructed local objects have their destructor called in case of an exception. This implies that if an exception occurs within an object's constructor, only its fully constructed data objects and base classes will have their destructors called. For example, in the following example, only the *TDataClass* and *TBaseClass* destructors are called.

```
//////////////////////////////////////////////////////
// XCPTCONS.CPP: Fully constructed objs are destroyed//
//////////////////////////////////////////////////////
#include <iostream.h>
#include <except.h>

class TDataClass
{
    public:
        TDataClass()
        {
            cout << "TDataClass::TDataClass()"
                << endl;
        }
```

```
        ~TDataClass()
         {
             cout << "TDataClass::~TDataClass()"
                  << endl;
         }
};

class TBaseClass
{
    public:
        TBaseClass()
         {
             cout << "TBaseClass::TBaseClass()"
                  << endl;
         }

        ~TBaseClass()
         {
             cout << "TBaseClass::~TBaseClass()"
                  << endl;
         }
};


class TDerivedClass : public TBaseClass
{
        TDataClass data;
    public:
        TDerivedClass()
         {
             cout << "TDerivedClass::TDerivedClass()"
                  << endl;
```

```cpp
            cout << "Throwing exception"
                    << endl;
            throw "Oops! Something's wrong...";
        }

        ~TDerivedClass()
        {
            cout << "TDerivedClass::~TDerivedClass()"
                    << endl;
        }
};


int main( void )
{
    try
    {
        TDerivedClass tdc;
        // ...
    }
    catch ( const char* msg )
    {
        cout << "Exception caught: "
                << msg
                << endl;

        return -1;
    }

    return 0;
}
```

The output of the program follows:

```
TBaseClass::TBaseClass()
TDataClass::TDataClass()
TDerivedClass::TDerivedClass()
Throwing exception
TDataClass::~TDataClass()
TBaseClass::~TBaseClass()
Exception caught: Oops! Something's wrong...
```

Use Local Objects To Represent Acquired Resources

To benefit from C++ exception handling, you must wrap resource initialization and cleanup in a class's constructor and destructor respectively and create local instances of the class when acquiring the resource. If a class's constructor allocates more than one type of resource or executes code that may throw an exception after a resource has been acquired, encapsulate each resource in its own class so that each allocated resource is always localized to a fully constructed local object.

Dynamic Objects

Destructor cleanup is restricted to fully constructed local objects. However, if an exception is thrown from the constructor of an object allocated with the *new* operator, the memory is automatically freed. See the following example:

```
//////////////////////////////////////////////////////////
// NEW_XCPT.CPP: Exception & dynamic objects...        //
//////////////////////////////////////////////////////////
#include <iostream.h>
```

```
//
// A simple class that throws an exception from
// its constructor...
//
class TVBClass
{
    public:
        TVBClass()
        {
            cout << "TVBClass::TVBClass()"
                    <<  endl;

            throw "Error in TVBClass' constructor";
        }
        ~TVBClass()
        {
            cout << "TVBClass::~TVBClass()"
                    <<  endl;
        }
};


//
// A class with TVBClass as a virtual base class
//
class TClass : public virtual TVBClass
{
        int i;
    public:
        TClass();
        ~TClass();
        void* operator new( size_t );
        void  operator delete( void *p );
};
```

```
TClass::TClass()
{
    cout << "TClass::TClass()" << endl;
}


TClass::~TClass()
{
    cout << "TClass::~TClass()" << endl;
}


void* TClass::operator new( size_t size )
{
    cout << "TClass::operator new() " << endl;
    return ::new char[size];
}


void TClass::operator delete( void *p )
{
    cout << "TClass::operator delete() " << endl;
    ::delete( p );
}


int main( void )
{
    TClass *tcp;

    try
    {
        //
        // Create dynamic instance of class
```

```
        // whose virtual base throws an
        // exception
        //
        tcp = new TClass;

        //
        // The following is never executed!
        //
        cout << "Object created..." << endl;
        delete tcp;
    }
    catch( const char *msg )
    {
        cout << "Exception: "
             << msg
             << endl;
    }

    return 0;
}
```

The output from the preceding code is

```
TClass::operator new()
TVBClass::TVBClass()
TClass::operator delete()
Exception: Error in TVBClass' constructor
```

Returning Values from Constructors and Destructors

C++ does not allow a constructor or destructor to return a value. However, you can use exceptions to report an error condition from an object's constructor or destructor. You can actually return more than just a value; you can return an object loaded with several data members and member functions.

For example,

```
/////////////////////////////////////////////////////////
// XCPT_CTR.CPP: 'Returning' value from constructor. //
/////////////////////////////////////////////////////////
#include <except.h>
#include <iostream.h>


class TSomeClass
{
        // ...
    public:
        struct xSomeClass
        {
            int errCode;
            xSomeClass( int err )
            {}
        };

        TSomeClass();
};


TSomeClass::TSomeClass()
{
    // ...
    if ( error_condition )
        throw xSomeClass( err_Code );
}


int main( void )
```

continues

continued

```
{
    try
    {
        TSomeClass tsc;
        // ...
    }
    catch( TSomeClass::xSomeClass& xinfo )
    {
        cout << "Exception error Code :"
             <<  xinfo.errCode
             <<  endl;
    }

    // Object successfully created!

    return 0;

}
```

Working with Exception Hierarchies

Because C++ exception handling allows you to provide a handler for a base class that automatically catches any objects publicly derived from the base class, related exceptions can often be grouped in a C++ hierarchy. By deriving the exception classes from a common base class, you can put polymorphism to work by catching a pointer or reference to the base in your handler. For example, the following classes can be used to represent I/O errors (see fig. 9.4).

Figure 9.4. *Classes used to represent I/O errors.*

The following code shows a possible implementation:

```cpp
///////////////////////////////////////////////////
// XCPTHIER.CPP: Sample Exception Hierarchy...      //
///////////////////////////////////////////////////
#include <iostream.h>

class TIOError
{
    public:
        virtual void explain()
        {
            // .. explain problem
        }
};


class TReadError : public TIOError
{
    public:
        void explain();
        // ...
};


class TWriteError : public TIOError
{
    public:
        void explain();
        // ...
};
```

```
int main( void )
{
    try
    {
        //
        // Do I/O
        //
    }
    catch( TIOError& ioerr )
    {
        ioerr.explain();
    }

    return 0;
}
```

Working with Predefined Exception Classes

There are a few predefined classes used by the C++ library to report exceptions. The following section looks at the *xmsg* and *xalloc* classes.

xmsg

The class *xmsg* is used to report messages about exceptions. It is declared as the following:

```
class _EXPCLASS xmsg
{
public:
    xmsg(const string _FAR &msg);
    xmsg(const xmsg _FAR &msg);
    ~xmsg();

    const string _FAR & why() const;
    void raise() throw(xmsg);
    xmsg& operator=(const xmsg _FAR &src);
private:
    string _FAR *str;
};
```

The following code shows throwing and catching an *xmsg*:

```
////////////////////////////////////////////////////
// XMSG_.CPP: Using xmsg to report exception msg...  //
////////////////////////////////////////////////////
#include <iostream.h>
#include <cstring.h>
#include <except.h>

void func()
{
    if ( something_is_wrong )
    {
        xmsg  xx( "Error encountered..." );
        throw xx;
    }
    // ...
}

int main( void )
{
```

```
    try
    {
        func();
        // ...
    }
    catch( xmsg& msg )
    {
        cerr << "Exception: "
            << msg.why()
            << endl;
        return -1;
    }

    return 0;
}
```

xalloc

The default new handler operator throws a *xalloc* exception when
operator new cannot allocate memory. The class is declared as follows:

```
class _EXPCLASS xalloc : public xmsg
{
public:
    xalloc(const string _FAR &msg, size_t size);
```

```
    size_t requested() const;
    void raise() throw(xalloc);
private:
    size_t siz;
};
```

You should enclose every memory allocation request in a *try-block* with a *catch(xalloc&)* handler.

```
/////////////////////////////////////////////////////
// NEWXLLC.CPP: Checking for xalloc when calling new.//
/////////////////////////////////////////////////////
#include <except.h>
#include <iostream.h>

void func()
{
    char *p = 0;

    try
    {
        p = new char[0x100];
    }
    catch( xalloc& xllc )
    {
        cerr << "xalloc caught.";
    }

    // ...
}
```

Bad_cast and Bad_typeid

A *Bad_cast* exception is thrown when *dynamic_cast* fails to cast a reference type. A *Bad_typeid* exception is thrown when the typeid operator is unable to identify its operand's type. For more information, see the Runtime Type Information chapter.

Using Exception Local Information

The header file *EXCEPT.H* defines three global variables that you can use to obtain information about an exception:

_*throwFileName*:	A character pointer to the name of the file from which the exception was thrown.
_*throwLineNumber*:	An unsigned variable with the line number in which the exception was thrown.
_*throwExceptionName*:	A character pointer to the name of the exception. That is, a pointer to a null-terminated string containing the type of object thrown.

Note: You must enable the compiler's Exception Local Information when accessing the filename and line number exception information variables. See Exceptions and Compiler Options for more information.

The following example accesses Exception Local Information:

```
///////////////////////////////////////////////////
// XCPTNAME.CPP: Using Exception Local Information.. //
///////////////////////////////////////////////////
#include <iostream.h>
#include <cstring.h>
#include <except.h>

void func( void )
{
    if ( error_cond )
    {
```

```cpp
        xmsg xx( "Error type: ###" );
        // ...
        throw xx;
    }
}


int main( void )
{
    try
    {
        func();
        // ...
    }
    catch( ... )
    {
        cout << "Exception type "
            << _ _throwExceptionName
            << " thrown: "
            << "Line #"
            << _ _throwLineNumber
            << " - File: "
            << _ _throwFileName
            << endl;

        return -1;
    }

    return 0;
}
```

The output for the preceding sample follows:

```
Exception type xmsg thrown: Line #14 - File: xcptname.cpp
```

Using Exceptions and Compiler Options

You can access the compiler settings related to C++ exception handling from the IDE by using the following steps:

1. Select the OPTIONS|PROJECT menu.

    The *Project Options* dialog appears.

2. Select and Expand the *C++ Options* Topic.

3. Select the Exception handling/RTTI SubTopic.

    The *Exception handling/RTTI* settings appear.

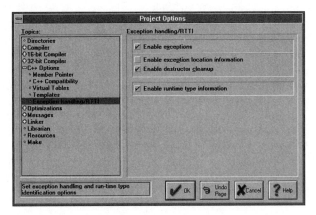

Figure 9.5. *C++ exception handling compiler options.*

The following table describes each setting and provides the equivalent command line options:

Table 9.1 Exception Handling Compiler Options

Option	Command Line	Description
Enable exceptions	-x	When disabled, the compiler generates an error message when it encounters a *try-block*. This option is enabled by default.
Enable exception location info.	-xp	When enabled, this option gives you access to filename and line number information about the *throw-point*. This option is disabled by default.
Enable destructor cleanup	-xd	This option allows the destructors of local objects created between the *throw-point* and the *handler* to be called. This option is enabled by default.

Examining Structured Exception Handling

Structured exception handling is actually part of the Windows NT operating system. When building a Win32 application, the Borland C++ compiler offers access to the OS's exception handling support with three new keywords: _ _try, _ _except, and _ _finally. Borland C++, however, makes *structured exception handling* available to code targeting 16-bit platforms. That is, the syntax described later is allowed in code targeting Windows and DOS applications, and the Borland C++ runtime library offers 16-bit versions of the various functions related to structured exception handling.

Structured exception handling offers two features: *frame-based exception handling* and *termination handling*. Frame-based exception handling allows you to specify a block of code that is executed if an exception occurs. Termination handling allows you to provide a block of code that is always executed irrespective of the flow of control.

Using Frame-based Exception Handling (_ _try/_ _except)

Frame-based exception handling involves three entities:

- First, there is a block of code following the _ _try keyword and enclosed by braces. The block is known as a *guarded body of code*. It is made up of one or more statements that may directly or indirectly raise an exception.

- Then, following the *guarded body of code* is the _ _except keyword that takes a *filter expression* as parameter.

- Finally, there's another block of code enclosed by braces and preceded by the _ _except keyword. This block is known as the *exception-handler block*. It is the block that handles exceptions.

The following shows the general syntax:

```
_ _try
{
        /* guarded body of code */
}
_ _except( expression filter )
{
        /* exception-handler block */
}
```

Raising an Exception

The *RaiseException( )* function can be used to raise an exception.

```
void
__cdecl __far
RaiseException(
    DWORD dwExceptionCode,
    DWORD dwExceptionFlags,
    DWORD nNumberOfArguments,
    const LPDWORD lpArguments
    );
```

dwExceptionCode:	Code identifying exception being raised.
dwExceptionFlags:	Specifies whether the exception is continuable. It can be either *EXCEPTION_CONTINUABLE* or *EXCEPTION_NONCONTINUABLE*.
nNumberOfArguments:	Specifies number of arguments passed in *lpArguments* array.
lpArguments:	Address of array of 32-bit arguments.

Flow of Control

If an exception is raised by a statement in the *guarded body of code*, the *filter-expression* is evaluated. The results of the evaluation determines the flow of control as shown in the following table:

Table 9.2 Possible Values of Filter Expression

Value	Description
EXCEPTION_EXECUTE_HANDLER	Control is transferred to *exception-handler block.*
EXCEPTION_CONTINUE_SEARCH	Control is not transferred to the associated *exception-handler block.* The stack is unwound, and the search for a handler continues.
EXCEPTION_CONTINUE_EXECUTION	The search for a handler is terminated, and control is returned to the location where the exception was raised.

The following example shows the _ _*try*, _ _*except* keywords and the *RaiseException* function:

```
/* ************************************************** */
/* SEH.C: Illustrates Structured Exception Handling..*/
/* ************************************************** */

#include <excpt.h>
#include <stdio.h>

#define EXCEPTION_ERROR_CODE 0x1000L


void doSomething( void )
{
    printf( "Trying to do something...\n" );
```

```c
    /* ---------------------------------- *\
    /* Let's assume something went wrong...*/
    /* So we'll raise an exception!        */

    printf( "Oops! Error encountered..\n" );
    printf( "Raising an exception.....\n" );

    RaiseException( EXCEPTION_ERROR_CODE,
                    EXCEPTION_CONTINUABLE,
                    0,      /*Param count...   */
                    0 );    /*Pointer to Param.*/
}


int main( void )
{
    try {
            doSomething();
        }

    except( EXCEPTION_EXECUTE_HANDLER )
        {
            printf( "Exception caught...\n" );
            return -1;
        }

    return 0;
}
```

Filter Expression

The *filter expression* often invokes a function called the *filter function*. The *filter function* commonly expects one or more parameters describing the exception and returns one of the three expected results of the *filter expression*. The *filter expression* and *exception-handler block* can obtain information regarding the exception by calling the following functions:

GetExceptionCode( ):   Returns the code identifying the exception raised.

GetExceptionInformation( ):   Returns a pointer to a structure containing detailed information about the exception.

The following example shows a *filter function*:

```
/* ************************************************* */
/* SEH_FLTR.C: Using a filter function...           */
/* ************************************************* */
#include <excpt.h>
#include <stdio.h>

#define  MY_EXCEPTION   0x0000FACE

void doSomething( void )
{
    /* Let's assume something went wrong...*/
    /* So we'll raise an exception!         */

    printf( "doSomething(): Error condition!\n" );
    printf( "RaisingException() \n" );

    RaiseException( MY_EXCEPTION, /* Code. */
                    EXCEPTION_CONTINUABLE,
```

```
                    0, /*Param count...    */
                    0);/*Pointer to Param..*/

    printf( "Guess, I must have been continued!" );
}


DWORD ExceptionFilter( DWORD dwCode )
{
    printf( "Exeption filter: Code=%ld\n", dwCode );

    if ( dwCode == MY_EXCEPTION )
        return EXCEPTION_EXECUTE_HANDLER;
    else
        return EXCEPTION_CONTINUE_SEARCH;

  /*-[NOTE]------------------------------------------*\
  ¦ You can also return EXCEPTION_CONTINUE_EXECUTION  ¦
  ¦ which returns control to where the exception occurred¦
  ¦ and stops searching for a handler...              ¦
  \*------------------------------------------------*/
}


int main( void )
{
    try {
            doSomething();
        }

    except( ExceptionFilter( GetExceptionCode() ) )
        {
            printf( "Exception caught...\n" );
        }

    return 0;
}
```

Catching Processor Exceptions

Frame-based exception handling can be used to catch processor exceptions when running under Windows NT (and partly under Win32s). For example, the notorious *general protection fault* can be handled using the *_try/_except* syntax. For these exceptions, the function *GetExceptionCode( )* returns one of the various constants defined in the header files *excpt.h* and *winbase.h*. A few of these constants follow:

```
EXCEPTION_ACCESS_VIOLATION
EXCEPTION_ARRAY_BOUNDS_EXCEEDED
EXCEPTION_FLT_DENORMAL_OPERAND
EXCEPTION_FLT_DIVIDE_BY_ZERO
EXCEPTION_FLT_INEXACT_RESULT
EXCEPTION_FLT_INVALID_OPERATION
EXCEPTION_FLT_OVERFLOW
EXCEPTION_FLT_STACK_CHECK
EXCEPTION_FLT_UNDERFLOW
EXCEPTION_INT_DIVIDE_BY_ZERO
EXCEPTION_INT_OVERFLOW
EXCEPTION_PRIV_INSTRUCTION
EXCEPTION_IN_PAGE_ERROR
EXCEPTION_ILLEGAL_INSTRUCTION
EXCEPTION_NONCONTINUABLE_EXCEPTION
EXCEPTION_STACK_OVERFLOW
EXCEPTION_INVALID_DISPOSITION
```

The following example shows how access violations can be handled via frame-based exception:

```
/* ************************************************* *\
¦ ACS_XCPT.C: Handling access violations...         ¦
¦                                                   ¦
¦                                                   ¦
¦   This sample will (at best) generate a 'Protection ¦
¦   violation' message if compiled, linked and     ¦
¦   executed as a 16-bit application. When compiled, ¦
¦   linked and executed as a 32-bit application, the ¦
```

```
¦    access violation caused by copying to a NULL      ¦
¦    pointer is elegantly handled via Frame-based       ¦
¦    Exception Handling...                              ¦
¦                                                       ¦
¦    To compile/link use the following command:         ¦
¦             BCC32   -W  -v   ACS_XCPT.C               ¦
\* ************************************************** */
#if !defined(STRICT)
#define       STRICT
#endif

#include <windows.h>
#include <excpt.h>
#include <string.h>


DWORD ExceptionFilter( DWORD dwCode,
                       EXCEPTION_POINTERS *pXcptInfo )
{
    if ( dwCode == STATUS_ACCESS_VIOLATION )
    {
        return EXCEPTION_EXECUTE_HANDLER;
    }
    else
    {
        return EXCEPTION_CONTINUE_SEARCH;
    }
}


int PASCAL WinMain( HINSTANCE hInstance,
                    HINSTANCE hPrevInstance,
                    LPSTR lpszCmdline,
                    int nCmdShow )
{
```

```
_ _try
{
    char *p = NULL;
    strcpy( p, "Oh la la!!" );
}
_ _except( ExceptionFilter( GetExceptionCode(),
                            GetExceptionInformation() ) )
{
    MessageBox( NULL,
                "Access Violation, terminating...",
                "Except-Handler-Code",
                MB_OK¦MB_TASKMODAL );
}
return 0;
}
```

Using Termination Handlers (_ _try/_ _finally)

Termination handling involves two components:

- First there is a block of code following the _ _try keyword and enclosed by braces. The block is known as a *guarded body of code*. It is made up of one or more statements that may directly or indirectly raise an exception.

- Then, following the *guarded body of code* is the _ _finally keyword followed by a block of code known as the *termination block*. The statements of the *termination block* are executed whenever control leaves the *guarded body of code*.

The following example shows the general syntax:

```
_ _try
{
        /* guarded body of code */
}
_ _finally
{
        /* termination block */
}
```

Normal versus Abnormal Termination

If control proceeds sequentially from the guarded body to the termination block, the guarded body is said to have terminated normally. An abnormal termination occurs when control leaves the guarded body because of

- a return, goto, break or continue statement
- a call to the *longjmp( )* function
- a raised exception

The *termination block* can call the *AbnormalTermination( )* function to find out how its *guarded body of code* was terminated.

The following example shows a termination handler:

```
/* ************************************************* */
/* TRM_HNDL.C: Using termination handlers...         */
/* ************************************************* */
```

```c
#include <stdio.h>
#include <excpt.h>


void func( void )
{
    /*
    Grab_A_Resource();
    */

    _ _try
    {
        /*
         Something goes wrong, Oops!
        */
        return;
    }
    _ _finally
    {
        /*
        Release_The_Resource();
        */
        printf( "_ _finally, guarded block terminated %s\n",
                AbnormalTermination() ?
                "abnormally" : "normally " );
    }
}


int main( void )
{
    func();
    return 0;
}
```

Combining Frame-Based and Termination Handlers

You can combine frame-based and termination handlers by nesting the blocks.

```
void funcA()              /* NOTE: If an exception is */
{                         /*       raised, the order  */
    _ _try                /*          of execution is: */
    {                     /* 1. Filter Expression     */
        _ _try            /* 2. Exception   Handler   */
        {                 /* 3. Termination Handler   */


            /* Guarded  Code... */
        }
        _ _except( filter_expression )
        {
            /* Exception Handler */
        }
    }
    _ _finally
    {
        /* Termination Handler */
    }
}


void funcB()              /* NOTE: If an exception is */
{                         /*       raised, the order  */
    _ _try                /*          of execution is: */
    {                     /* 1. Filter Expression     */
        _ _try            /* 2. Termination Handler   */
        {                 /* 3. Exception   Handler   */
```

continues

continued

```
        /* Guarded  Code...  */
    }
    _ _finally
    {
        /* Termination Hndlr */
    }
}
_ _except( filter_expression )
{
    /* Exception Handler    */
}
}
```

Using Structured and C++ Exception Handling

- C++ Exception handling (*try/throw/catch*) cannot be used in a C module.

- Similarly, the termination handling syntax (*_ _try/_ _finally*) cannot be used in a C++ module.

- A C frame-based handler can be used in a C++ module. Use the *try/ _ _except* or *try/except* keyword pair when implementing a C frame-base handler in a C++ module.

Summary

In this chapter, you've seen the features available to programmers with exception handling. These have included a consistent mechanism for reporting and handling error conditions and the ability to ensure that resources are returned to the system when unexpected conditions are encountered at runtime. Several components of the C++ runtime support libraries (eg. operator new, ANSI C++ *string* class) use exception handling, and this trend is likely to continue as the ANSI/ISO C++ committee shapes the details of C++. So take advantage of the mechanism and *catch* the wave!

Chapter 10
Runtime Type Information and Typecast Operators

Runtime Type Information (RTTI) is a mechanism that allows you to determine the type of an object at runtime. This is especially useful in a class hierarchy in which a pointer or reference to a base object is often pointing to or aliasing an instance of a class derived from the base class. With the facility to identify an object's type comes the ability to perform safe casts. In other words, by making use of type information it is possible to check and only allow safe and meaningful casts. This chapter looks at the implementation, syntax, and use of RTTI as well as the new style casts of C++. Although these features are relatively new additions to the C++ language, they'll help you resolve old problems or limitations, such as casting from a virtual base class to a derived class.

Programming with RTTI

RTTI is not implemented for every C++ type, but only for classes with one or more virtual functions (i.e. *polymorphic types*). The syntax, however, can still be used with non-polymorphic types (including built-in types such as 'char' or 'double') although the identification is then static and not dynamic. The following section looks at the syntax for using RTTI.

Using typeid Operator and Type_info Class

RTTI is accessible via an operator and a class:

- The new *typeid* operator takes a type-name or an expression as parameter and returns a reference to an object of type *Type_info*.

  Syntax:

  ```
  typeid( type_name )
              typeid( expression)
  ```

  Result:

  ```
  const Type_info&
  ```

- The class *Type_info*, defined in the header file *typeinfo.h,* holds information about a type.

When passed an expression that represents a reference or a pointer to a polymorphic type, the typeid operator examines the object at runtime and returns its dynamic type information. When passed an expression representing a reference or pointer to a non-polymorphic type, the *typeid* operator returns a *Type_info&* object representing the static type of the expression (in other words, the expression and not the type of object referenced or pointed to is examined).

Bad_typeid Exception

A *Bad_typeid* exception is thrown if the *typeid* operator fails to identify the type of its operand.

Using typeid To Compare Types

You can use the *typeid* operator to compare the types of objects at runtime. The following code shows object type comparisons. Note the difference between polymorphic and non-polymorphic types:

```
/////////////////////////////////////////////////////////
// TYPECMP1.CPP: Comparing types using typeid...     //
/////////////////////////////////////////////////////////
#include <iostream.h>
#include <typeinfo.h>

//
// Non-polymorphic type
//
class TBase1
{
    public:
    // ...
};
```

```
//
// Non-polymorphic type
//
class TDerived1 : public TBase1
{
    public:
    // ...
};


int main( void )
{
    TDerived1 d;
    TBase1    &br= d;

    cout << "typeid(br) "
        << (typeid(br) == typeid(TBase1) ? "==" : "!=")
        << " typeid(TBase1)"
        << endl;

    cout << "typeid(br) "
        << (typeid(br) == typeid(TDerived1) ? "==" : "!=")
        << " typeid(TDerived1)"
        << endl;

    return 0;
}
```

The preceding sample's output is

```
typeid(br) == typeid(TBase1)
typeid(br) != typeid(TDerived1)
```

Error! Bookmark not defined. TBase1 is non-polymorphic. Although *br*
is actually aliasing a *TDerived1* class, the preceding result shows its type
as *TBase1**.

```cpp
//////////////////////////////////////////////////////////
// TYPECMP2.CPP: Comparing types using typeid...     //
//////////////////////////////////////////////////////////
#include <iostream.h>
#include <typeinfo.h>


//
// Polymorphic type
//
class TBase2
{
    public:
        virtual ~TBase2()
            {}
    // ...
};



//
// Polymorphic type
//
class TDerived2 : public TBase2
{
    public:
    // ...
};




int main( void )
{
    TDerived2 d;
    TBase2    &br= d;
```

```
    cout << "typeid(br) "
        << (typeid(br) == typeid(TBase2) ? "==" : "!=")
        << " typeid(TBase2)"
        << endl;

    cout << "typeid(br) "
        << (typeid(br) == typeid(TDerived2) ? "==" : "!=")
        << " typeid(TDerived2)"
        << endl;

    return 0;
}
```

The above sample's output is:

```
typeid(br) != typeid(TBase2)
typeid(br) == typeid(TDerived2)
```

Now TBase2 is polymorphic. So, *br* is correctly identified as aliasing an instance of the *TDerived2* class.

Using Type_info

The following is a slightly edited version of the *Type_info* class declaration:

```
class  __rtti  Type_info
{
  public:

      tpid    __far *        tpp;
```

```
private:
                __cdecl Type_info(const Type_info _FAR &);
    Type_info & __cdecl operator=(const Type_info _FAR &);

public:

    virtual  __cdecl ~Type_info();

    int  __cdecl operator==(const Type_info _FAR &) const;
    int  __cdecl operator!=(const Type_info _FAR &) const;

    int  __cdecl before(const Type_info _FAR &) const;

    const char _FAR *__cdecl name() const;
};
```

- The copy constructor and assignment operator are private to ensure that instances of *Type_info* are not accidentally created or copied.

- The virtual destructor makes *Type_info* polymorphic.

- The overloaded == and *!=* operators allow you to compare two *Type_info* objects (compare the results of calls to the *typeid* operator) as shown in the preceding *TYPECMP1.CPP* and *TYPECMP2.CPP* code.

Type_info::before(const Type_info&)

The *before( )* method of *Type_info* is implementation-dependent and reflects an ordered sequence among types. The Borland C++ version of *before* simply performs a literal comparison of the name of the two types involved.

```
if ( typeid( TypeA ).before( typeid( TypeB ) ) )
```

is equivalent to

```
if ( strcmp( typeid( TypeA ).name( ),
             typeid( TypeB ).name( ) ) < 0 )
```

Type_info::name()

The *name()* method of *Type_info* returns a string representing the name of the type described by the *Type_info* object.

Using RTTI and Compiler Options

RTTI is enabled with Borland C++ by default. If you use the IDE, you can configure this Compiler setting by using the following steps:

1. Select the OPTIONS|PROJECT menu.

   The *Project Options* dialog appears.

2. Select and expand the *C++ Options* topic.

3. Select the Exception handling/RTTI subTopic.

   The *Exception handling/RTTI* settings appear.

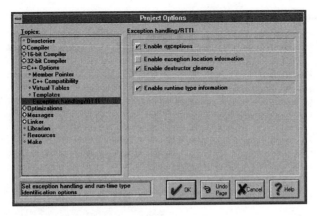

Figure 10.1. *RTTI Compiler options.*

Command Line users can use the *-RT* option (enabled by default) to explicitly enable RTTI. Using *-RT-* disables RTTI.

Using the _ _*rtti* Modifier

You can ensure that RTTI is generated for a class regardless of the compiler setting by using the _ _*rtti* modifier when declaring the class. For example:

```
class _ _rtti TClass
{
    public:
        virtual ~TClass();  // Polymorphic!
};
```

Using RTTI

Although RTTI offers great flexibility, it should NOT be used in place of virtual functions. For example, the following code illustrates an incorrect use of RTTI.

```
#include <typeinfo.h>

class TBaseWnd{  public: virtual ~TBaseWnd();  };
class TMainWnd : public  TBaseWnd {};
class TDlgWnd  : public  TBaseWnd {};

void Create( TBaseWnd *pWnd )
{
    //
    // Very costly use of RTTI - use of virtual
    // functions is more elegant and involves
    // less overhead!!
    //
    if      ( typeid(pWnd) == typeid(TMainWnd) )
        CreateWindow(...);
    else if ( typeid(pWnd) == typeid(TDlgWnd)  )
        CreateDialog(...);
    else

    // ...
}
```

Use RTTI when you've extended a library class by derivation and it was not possible or meaningful to add virtual functions in the base classes of the hierarchy. See the following example code:

```
#include <typeinfo.h>

class TMyMainWnd : public TMainWnd
{
```

```
    public:
        virtual void myUniqueMethod();
};


void WindowActivated( TBaseWnd *pActiveWnd )
{
    if ( typeid(pActiveWnd) == typeid(TMyMainWnd) )
        ((TMyMainWnd*)pActiveWnd)->myUniqueMethod();

    // ...
}
```

In other words, use RTTI when the type of an object cannot be
determined at compile time and other C++ mechanisms such as late
binding cannot be implemented to provide proper handling of the
respective types.

Using New Style Casts

Borland C++ supports the new cast syntax including the *dynamic_cast*
operator. The *dynamic_cast* operator takes advantage of RTTI to allow
safe conversions that are checked at runtime. The following section
looks at the syntax and purpose of these new typecast operators.

Examining New Style Casts

Section 5.4 of the Annotated C++ Reference Manual (ARM) mentions the following about the traditional cast notation used for explicit type conversion:

> "Explicit type conversion is often best avoided. Using a cast suppresses the type checking provided by the compiler and will therefore lead to surprises unless the programmer really was right."

In other words, the traditional cast notation allows the programmer to (unintentionally) perform unverified type conversions that fail at runtime.

Another shortcoming of the traditional cast notation is that the syntax does not reflect the programmer's real intent. For example, a cast may be used if the programmer needs to

- Alter the way the compiler looks at a memory location without modifying the latter. In the following example the cast of i to type *unsigned* completely changes the result of the *if* statement:

```
int i = -2;

if ( i < -1 )
    cout << "i < -1"
        << endl;

if ( unsigned(i) < -1 )
    cout << "i < -1"
        << endl;
```

- Alter the actual outcome of an evaluation. In the following example the address passed in the second call to function *Call4Msg( )* is different from the first call because of the cast.

```
#include <iostream.h>

class A
{
    public:
        virtual void msg();
};

class B : public virtual A
{
    public:
        void msg();
};

class C : public virtual A
{
    public:
        void msg();
};

class D : public B, public C
{
    public:
        void msg();
};

void Call4Msg( A* ap )
{
    ap->msg();
}

int main( void )
{
    D d;
```

```
        Call4Msg( &d );
        Call4Msg( &(C)d );

        return 0;
}
```

- Eliminate a compile time error message. See the following example:

```
const int TblSize = 0x100;

const int *iTbl;

void CreateTbl( void )
{
    int *ip = new int[TblSize];
    // ...
    iTbl = ip;
}

void DestroyTbl( void )
{
    delete [] ( int* )iTbl;
}
```

The cast to *int** is required when calling *operator delete*. Otherwise, the error message Cannot convert 'const int*' to 'void *' in function DestroyTbl() is generated.

The traditional cast notation also suffers from another limitation: a pointer to a base class *B* cannot be explicitly converted to a pointer to a derived class *D* if *B* is a virtual base class. See the following example:

```
class A {};                            //          A
class B : public virtual A   {};       //        /   \
class C : public virtual A   {};       //       B     C
class D : public B, public C {};       //        \   /
                                       //          D
```

```
void func( A *ap )
{
    //
    // The following line generates the error message:
    //      "Cannot cast from 'A *' to
    //        'D *' in function func(A *)"
    //
    D* dp = (D*)ap;
    // ...
}

int main( void )
{
    D d;
    func( &d );
    // ...
    return 0;
}
```

The new style casts solve the problems of the traditional cast by

- Providing a clear and distinct syntax which documents the programmer's intent.

- Supplying both compile-time and run-time error detection.

- Eliminating the inability to convert a virtual base class pointer to a pointer of a type derived from the base class.

Using dynamic_cast

The *dynamic_cast* typecast operator allows you to perform safe type conversions: when casting polymorphic objects, the validity of the conversion is checked at runtime.

Syntax:

dynamic_cast<T>(v)

where:

T is a reference type, a pointer type or *void**.

v is a reference if *T* is a reference type; otherwise *v* is a pointer.

The result of operator *dynamic_cast* is of type *T* unless the conversion fails. Upon failure, *dynamic_cast*

- Throws a *Bad_cast* exception if *T* is a reference.

- Returns a null pointer if *T* is a pointer.

Note: *dynamic_cast* requires RTTI. So make sure that:

- *v* is a polymorphic type

- the RTTI option is enabled when compiling

Looking at a *dynamic_cast* Example

The following example constrasts the traditional cast style and the *dynamic_cast* operator:

```
///////////////////////////////////////////////////
// DYN_CAST.CPP: Using the dynamic_cast operator...   //
///////////////////////////////////////////////////
#include <iostream.h>

//
// Lets assume TAppObject is a fully functional
// class available from a Library or Framework.
//
class TAppObject
```

```
{
    public:
        virtual ~TAppObject(){}
        // ...
};



//
// The GetAppObject() function returns a
// pointer to the process' TAppObject.
//
TAppObject* GetAppObject( void );



//
// Let's say we need to enhance the TAppObject
// class and therefore create a new class
// derived from TAppObject where we override
// some of TAppObject's methods, add new data
// members and new member functions.
//
class TMyAppObject : public TAppObject
{
        // ...
    public:
        virtual void myMethod();
        // ...
};



//
// This function illustrates the traditional [dangerous]
// cast notation as well as the safer new cast style...
//
void func()
{
```

```
#if !defined(__USE_CHECKED_CAST)

    //
    // Here we use the old style of casting.
    //

    TMyAppObject*
    objPtr = (TMyAppObject*)GetAppObject();

    //
    // If 'objPtr' is not really pointing to an
    // instance of 'TMyAppObject', the following
    // call will fail miserably!
    //
    objPtr->myMethod();

    // ...

#else

    //
    // Here we use the new/safe style of casting
    //

    TMyAppObject*
    objPtr = dynamic_cast<TMyAppObject*>(GetAppObject());

    if ( objPtr )    // Confirm validity of cast!
    {
        objPtr->myMethod();

        // ...
    }

#endif
}
```

Downcasting from a Virtual Base Class

With the traditional cast notation, the C++ language does not allow conversion from a virtual base class to a derived class. However, with the information available via RTTI, you can downcast from a virtual base using the *dynamiccast* operator as long as the class is *polymorphic* and the conversion is unambiguous. See the following example:

```
/////////////////////////////////////////////////////
// VB_DNCST.CPP: dynamic_cast & virtual base class.  //
/////////////////////////////////////////////////////
#include <iostream.h>
#include <typeinfo.h>

class A
{
    public:             //
        virtual ~A(){}  // RTTI's only supported
                        // for polymorphic types.
};                      //

class B : public virtual A    {};
class C : public virtual A    {};
class D : public B, public C {};

void func( A& refA )
{
```

```
    try
    {
        D &d = dynamic_cast<D&>( refA );
        //
        // Use d ...
        //
    }
    catch( Bad_cast& )
    {
        cout << "Bad_cast caught..."
            << endl;
    }
}


int main( void )
{
    D d;
    func( d );
    // ...
    return 0;
}
```

Cross-Hierarchy Casting

The *dynamic_cast* operator allows *cross-hierarchy* casting; that is, you can safely convert between classes that seem totally unrelated at compile time. Consider the following hierarchy, shown in figure 10.2.

Figure 10.2. *Cross-hierarchy casting.*

If the traditional casting notation is used to convert an input pointer to an output pointer:

- The conversion is allowed although it is most likely invalid.

- The result of the conversion is unusable (even if it was valid) because no pointer adjustment is done.

The *dynamic_cast* operator, however, can be used to

- Verify the validity of the conversion.

- Perform the conversion with the necessary pointer adjustment.

See the following for an example:

```
///////////////////////////////////////////////////
// XHIERCST.CPP: Cross-Hierarchy casting...        //
///////////////////////////////////////////////////
#include <iostream.h>

class Input
{
    public:
        virtual void readData();
};


class Output
{
    public:
        virtual void writeData();
};
```

```
class IO_Object : public Input, public Output
{
};


void func( Input *pi )
{
    //
    // Maybe pi is really pointing
    // to an IO_Object!! Let's see...
    //
    Output *po = dynamic_cast<Output*>(pi);
    if ( po )
        po->writeData();

    // ...
}


int main( void )
{
    Input i;
    func( &i );

    IO_Object io;
    func( &io );

    // ...

    return 0;
}
```

Using static_cast

The *static_cast* operator can be used to perform conversions between

- integral types
- integral and floating types
- integral and enum types
- pointers and references to objects within a hierarchy provided the conversion is unambiguous and does not involve downcasting a virtual base class.

Syntax:

static_cast<T>(v)

where:

T is a pointer, reference, arithmetic, or enum type.

v evaluates to an instance of a pointer, reference, arithmetic, or enum type.

The result of operator *static_cast* is of type *T*.

The following example illustrates the use of the *static_cast* operator:

```
///////////////////////////////////////////////////
// STA_CAST.CPP: Using the static_cast operator...  //
///////////////////////////////////////////////////

void func( void )
{
    int    i;
    long   l;
    //
```

```
// (  Integral <-> Integral  )
//
l = static_cast<long>(i);


float f;
//
// (  Floating <-> Integral  )
//
f = static_cast<float>(i);


char c;
enum Managers { Matt, Jen, Jerry, Georgia, Jeff };
Managers mgr;
//
// (  enum <-> Integral  )
//
c = static_cast<char>(mgr);

}
```

The *static_const* operator can be used to convert between base and derived pointers (references) of a hierarchy. The conversion is performed at compile-time.

```
class Base  {};
class Derived : public Base {};

void func( void )
{
    Derived d;
```

```
    //  (  Derived -> Base  )
    Base *bp = static_cast<Base*>(&d);


    Base b;
    //  (  Base -> Derived  )
    Derived &dr = static_cast<Derived&>(b);

    //  ...
}
```

dynamic_cast versus static_cast

Both *dynamic_cast* and *static_cast* can be used when converting pointers and references within a hierarchy. *dynamic_cast* is the preferred method because

- *dynamic_cast* is safer, especially when downcasting.

- *dynamic_cast* does not add any overhead if the conversion can safely be performed at compile time. In other words, *dynamic_cast* will generate the same code as *static_cast* whenever it's reliable to do so.

- *dynamic_cast* allows downcasting from a virtual base class.

- *dynamic_cast* validates and performs correct cross-hierarchy casting.

However, you must use *static_cast* instead of *dynamic_cast* when converting pointers or references of non-polymorphic classes.

Using const_cast

The *const_cast* operator can be used to remove or add the *const* or *volatile* type qualifiers.

Syntax:

const_cast<T>(v)

where:

T is a type.

v evaluates to an instance of same type as *T* except for *const* and *volatile* modifiers.

The result of operator *const_cast* is of type *T*.

The following example illustrates the *const_cast* typecast operator:

```
/////////////////////////////////////////////////////
// CNST_CST.CPP: Using the const_cast operator...    //
/////////////////////////////////////////////////////
const int TblSize = 0x100;
const int *iTbl;

void CreateTbl( void )
{
    int *ip = new int[TblSize];
    // ...
    iTbl = ip;
}

void DestroyTbl( void )
{
    delete [] const_cast<int*>(iTbl);
}
```

Using reinterpret_cast

The *reinterpret_cast* operator can be used to change the way the compiler sees an object's type; however, the operator does not modify the object.

Syntax:

> reinterpret_cast<T>(v)

> *T* can be a pointer, reference, integral (char, short, int, long, enumerations) or floating (float, double, long double) type.

> *v* can be an instance of a pointer/reference type or an integral or floating type variable if *T* is a pointer/reference. *v* can be a pointer/reference instance if *T* is an integral or floating type.

The result of operator *const_cast* is of type *T*.

You can use *reinterpret_cast* to convert an integral type to a pointer or vice-versa. For example:

```
#include <windows.h>

void func()
{
    DWORD  dwData;
    LPSTR  lpszStr;

    dwData  = reinterpret_cast<DWORD>(lpszStr);
    lpszStr = reinterpret_cast<LPSTR>(dwData );
    // ...
}
```

You can also use *reinterpret_cast* to convert from one pointer type to another as long as no adjustment is necessary. Therefore *reinterpret_cast* should not be used when converting between pointers of objects within a hierarchy.

> **Note:** The compiler will NOT generate an error message if you use
> *reinterpret_cast* to convert between base class and derived class
> pointers/references. The result, however, will be incorrect. For
> example:
>
> ```
> // Legal but incorrect!
> Derived *dp = reinterpret_cast<Derived*>(a_base_ptr);
> ```

Summary

Like exception handling, RTTI is a relatively new addition to the C++
language that allows for safer and more robust applications. The new
typecast operators help by validating explicit conversions and clarifying
their intent. Of course, the implementation of these innovations involves
some overhead but when properly applied, the advantages outweigh the
drawbacks.

Appendix A
Name Mangling Scheme of Borland C++

Name-mangling is the basis of *function overloading* and *type-safe linkage*. The C++ compiler mangles (or decorates) the names of functions and class-member functions to reflect the following:

- The class the function belongs to (in the case of member functions)

- The name of the function or the function type in the case of constructors, destructors, overloaded operators, or conversion functions

- The argument types expected by the function

The following section examines the way name-mangling is implemented in Borland C++. Understanding the name-mangling scheme is useful when investigating the causes of `Undefined symbol` *xxxx* `in module` `fname.ext` error messages in a C++ application. The explanation for these errors often is related to *name mangling*. A good grasp of the implementation also is helpful if you intend to write C++ methods or overloaded functions in assembly language.

General Overview of Scheme

The general format of a mangled name is

`@[classname@]EncodedFuncName$qEncodedArgType`

where:

- *classname* is the class name (when mangling class-member functions).

- *EncodedFuncName* is the function name. If the function is a constructor, destructor, overloaded operator, or conversion function, a special *EncodedFuncName* is used.

- *EncodedArgType* is a pattern encoding the argument types expected by the function.

@[classname@]

Every mangled name starts with the letter @. For class members, the name of the class and another @ character follows the initial @ letter.

EncodedFuncName

The *EncodedFuncName* is typically the function's name unless the function is a constructor, destructor, overloaded operator, or conversion function. The following table describes the encoding scheme used for these functions:

Table A.1 Function Encoding

Function Type	Encoding	Comments
Constructor	$bctr	
Destructor	$bdtr	
Conversion Function	$o	
Overloaded Operator	$bxxx	where xxx represents the overloaded operator as shown in the Overloaded Operator Encoding Table that follows.

Table A.2 Overloaded Operator Encoding

Overloaded Operator	Encoding
+	add
&	adr
&	and
->	arow
->*	arwm

continues

Overloaded Operator	Encoding
=	asg
( )	call
~	cmp
'	coma
--	dec
delete	dele
/	div
==	eql
>=	geq
>	gtr
++	inc
*	ind
&&	land
||	lor
<=	leq
<<	lsh
<	lss
%	mod
*	mul
!=	neq

Overloaded Operator	Encoding
new	new
!	not
|	or
&=	rand
/=	rdiv
<<=	rlsh
-=	rmin
%=	rmod
*=	rmul
|=	ror
+=	rplu
>>=	rrsh
^=	rxor
-	sub
[]	subs
^	xor

$qEncodedArgType

The *EncodedArgType* is a character sequence that represents the arguments expected by the function. The encoding contains the argument types and their modifiers. The following table shows the characters used for the various modifiers.

Table A.3 Encoding of Type Modifiers

Modifier	Encoding
Far reference	m
Far pointer	n
Near reference	r
Near pointer	p
Huge pointer	up
Segment pointer	ur
unsigned	u
signed	z
const	x
volatile	w

The bulk of the *EncodedArgType* reflects the argument types expected by the function. The following table shows the type encoding.

Table A.4 Encoding of Types

Type	Encoding
char	c
double	d
ellipsis	e
float	f
long double	g
int	i
long	l
short	s
void	v

User-Defined Types and Arrays

User-defined types such as enumeration or classes are mangled to a decimal count followed by the type name. The count indicates the length of the type name. Array types are preceded with an *a* followed by the array size and the type name.

Appendix B
RTL Helper Functions

The Borland Runtime Library offers more than an array of user-callable functions. The RTL contains a set of routines, commonly known as *helper functions* that the compiler makes use of when processing your C or C++ modules. When encountering certain C or C++ constructs, the Borland C++ compiler may choose to call a predefined routine instead of generating in-line instructions. For example, in the following snippet the compiler invokes a special routine to perform the division of longs:

```
#include <time.h>
#include <iostream.h>

int main()
{
    time_t secsPassed = time(NULL);
    time_t minsPassed = secsPassed/60;

    cout << "Minutes since 1/1/1970: "<<minsPassed
        << endl;

    return 0;
}
```

If the Check stack overflow option is enabled, the compiler also generates a call to another helper function that checks for stack overflow.

This appendix documents a few areas in which the Borland C++ compiler takes advantage of helper functions. It is important to understand that helper functions are for the compiler's use! You should not call any helper functions directly. However, a general understanding of how and when they are used can be very useful. You may encounter helper functions during a debugging session while viewing the CPU window or looking at a call stack. You also can improve the performance of your application by avoiding constructs that result in less than optimal use of helper functions.

Generating Assembly Language Output Files

One of the best methods to examine the code generated by Borland C++ is to enable the Generate Assembler Source compiler option. The assembly language output files generated by the compiler include your C or C++ source lines as comments. The following is an excerpt of the assembly language output file generated for the preceding code snippet:

```
;
; {
;       time_t secsPassed = time(NULL);
;
  push 0
  push 0
  call far ptr _time
  add  sp,4
  mov  word ptr [bp-4],dx
  mov  word ptr [bp-6],ax
;
;       time_t minsPassed = secsPassed/60;
;
  push 0
  push 60
  push word ptr [bp-4]
  push word ptr [bp-6]
  call far ptr F_LDIV@
```

The assembler output file reveals that the compiler makes use of the *F_LDIV@* function for the division.

Allocation Arrays of Classes

If you allocate an array of classes with constructors, the compiler calls a helper function that first allocates memory for the array and then initializes its contents by invoking the constructor for each element.

```
static int defaultX = -1
static int defaultY = -1

class Point
{
    public:
        Point( int _x=defaultX, int _y=defaultY)
        : x(_x), y(_y)
        {}
        // ...
    private:
        int x, y;
};

const int numPoints = 100;
int main( void )
{
    Point *ppt = new Point[numPoints];

    /*
     * ...
     */
```

```
        delete []ppt;
        return 0;
}
```

The dynamic allocation of an array Point used in the preceding sample code results in a call to the helper function vector_new_ as shown in the following assembly language listing:

```
; {
;        Poit *ppt = new Point[numPoints];
;
    push seg @Point@$bctr$qv
    push offset @Point@$bctr$qv
    push 5
    push 0
    push 100
    push 4
    push 0
    push 0
    call far ptr @_vector_new_$qnvuivluie
    add sp,16
```

Copying Structures

When processing the assignment of structures, Borland C++ may make use of the SCOPY@ helper function. This function matches the behavior of the ANSI C memcpy: it copies a specified number of bytes from a *source* to a *destination*.

The following sample illustrates a case in which understanding help function usage can help you fine-tune your application:

```
struct structA
{
    int accoutn;
    char code;
};

struct structB
{
    int accoutn;
    int code;
};

structA al, a2={ 100, 'x' };
structB b1, b2={ 100, 0  };

int main( void )
{
    a1 = a2;
    b1 = b2;

    return 0;
}
```

The first assignment of *a2* to *a1* results in a call to a helper function:

```
    ; int main( void )
    ;
        assume    cs:SCOPY_TEXT,ds:DGROUP
_main       proc far
    ;
    ; {
    ;       a1 = a2;
    ;
        push ds
        push offset DGROUP:_al
        push ds
```

```
    push offset DGROUP:_a2
    mov  cx,3
    call far ptr F_SCOPY@
;
```

The assignment of *b2* to *b1*, however, is performed with in-line code:

```
;        b1 = b2;
;
    mov dx,word ptr DGROUP:_b2+2
    mov ax,word ptr DGROUP:_b2
    mov word ptr DGROUP:_b1+2,dx
    mov word ptr DGROUP:_b1,ax
;
```

By comparing *structA* and *structB*, you will notice that their sizes differ by one byte. Therefore, the call to the helper function can be eliminated by padding *structA*. You also can eliminate the use of the helper function by enabling the speed optimizations of Borland C++.

Checking for Stack Overflow

The *Test Stack Overflow* compiler option instructs the compiler to perform a runtime check for stack overflow at the entry of each function compiled. Actually, the compiler generates a call to a helper function that carries out the task. The following assembly language listings illustrate the effect of the *Test Stack Overflow* option for a simple function that returns a constant value.

```
double pie()
{
    return 22/7;
}
```

```
; Check Stack Ovrflw: OFF         ;Check Stack Ovrflw:  ON
;                                 ;
; double pie()                     ; double pie()
;                                 ;
@pie$qv proc far                 @pie$qv proc far
 inc bp                           inc bp
push bp                          push bp
mov bp,sp                        mov bp,sp
                                 xor ax,ax
                                 call far ptr F_CHKSTK@

;                                 ;
; {                               ; {
;        return 22/7;             ;        return 22/7;
;                                 ;
fld dword ptr DGROUP:s@          fld dword ptr DGROUP:s@
jmp short @1@58                  jmp short @1@58
@1@58:                           @1@58:
;                                 ;
; }                               ; }
;                                 ;
```

Summary

Borland C++ makes use of many other helper functions when compiling your C and C++ code. The sources to most of these functions are included with the Borland C++ Runtime Library sources. You should not make any direct calls to these functions. Understanding their usage, however, will help you understand the code generated by the compiler.

Index

Symbols

-K2 switch, 25

-U command-line option, undefining macros, 94

. operator, 189

.* operator, 192

/*, comment signifier, C language, 35

//, comment signifier, C++ language, 35

::, scope resolution operator, 162-163, 187

<<, (left-shift operator), ostream class, 251

= operator, 201

>>, (right-shift operator), istream class, 251

@[classname@], mangled names, 430

[] operator, overloading, 216-219

\, (backslash) as line continuation character, 93

\, escape character in C language, 46-47

_ _cplusplus macro, 179

_ _except keyword, 386

_ _finally keyword, 394

_ _rtti modifier, RTTI, 409

_ _try keyword, 386, 394

_ _asm keyword, 141-144

_ _cdecl modifier, 137

_ _cs keyword, 127

_ _ds keyword, 127

_ _es keyword, 127

_ _export modifier, 136

_ _far keyword, 122, 129-131

_ _fastcall modifier, 139-140

_ _FILE_ _ macro, 103

_ _huge modifier, 131

_ _interrupt modifier, 133

_ _LINE_ _ macro, 103

_ _loadds modifier, 136

_ _near keyword, 122

_ _pascal modifier, 138-139

_ _saveregs modifier, 136

_ _seg modifier, 128

_ _ss keyword, 127

_ _ss modifier, 127

_BIG_INLINE macro, 253

{}, (braces for blocks), 56

~, (tilde, destructors of classes, 182, 204

16-bit DOS and Windows environments, Borland C++ extensions for, 117

A

AbnormalTermination( ) function, 395-398

abort( ) function, 363

abstract classes, 243-245

access specifiers of classes, 184-185

access violations and frame-based exception handling, 392-394

accessing data members, 190

Add Node menu option, 9

Add Target dialog box, 13

Add to Project List dialog box, 10

addresses
    descriptor tables for in Windows, 119
    far/near pointers to, 121-122
    selectors for in Windows, 119

Advanced button
    Add Target dialog box, 13
    New Project dialog box, 9

B

C

const variables in Borland C++ language, 167

const_cast operator, 426

constant_expression in C language, 60

constants
    C language, 37-39
    macros, 39
    manifest, 92
    symbolic, 92
    typed in C language, 41

constream class, 305

constructors, 196-200
    calling with placement syntax, 197
    classes, 182
    conversion, 209-210
    exceptions, 366-374
    file stream, 278-286
    ifstream, 279
    inheritance, 230-231
    ofstream, 279
    overloaded, 213
    returning values from, 372-374

continue statement in C language, 67

conversion
    between base and derived pointers with static_, 424
    constructors, 209-210
    functions, 209
    routines, 210
    specifications, 43-45

copy constructors, 200-201
    assignment operator, 203
    exception types, 358-360
    private, 201

copying structures, 441-443

CopyString function, 62

cout object, 250

_ _cplusplus macro, 179

.CPP file extensions source files, 2

CPP.EXE utility, 91

CPU registers and flags and pseudo registers, 144-145

cross-hierarchy casting, 420-422

CS (code segment), 118

_ _cs keyword, 127

CS register, 118

customizing project window for node views, 34

D

data abstraction with return type references, 159

data members
    accessing, 190
    classes, 186
    const/reference, 199
    static, 219-220
    static public, 220

data types
    C language, 39-40
    redefining, 81-82
    user-defined, 81-88

Debug menu commands
    Run, 7
    Run command, 10

debugging macros, 95

declarations
    functions in C language, 49-50
    Type_info class, 406-408
    type names for variables, 167
    variables in Borland C++ language, 166

F

N

O

P

Q–R

querying stream status, 276-277

RaiseException( ) function, 386-389

.rc files (resource scripts), 10

read function (iostream library), 289-290

reading strings, 294-297

readLong function, 51

recompiling C as C++, 148-151

Rect class, 184

redefining data types, 81-82

reference data member, 199

reference parameters, 156-158

reference variables, 156

references
   & operator, 154-155
   extern, 155
   passing arguments by, 158
   function templates, 322
   return type, 159
   returning to objects, 201
   virtual mechanism, 233

registers
   CPU, 144-145
   CS, 118
   DS, 119
   ES, 119
   SP (Stack Pointer), 346
   SS, 119

reinterpret_cast operator, 427-428

renamed global variable versions, 28-29

resolving references for function templates, 322

resource compilers/linkers, 22-23

resource scripts (.rc files), 10

restrictions
   on function overloading, 164
   on inline functions, 161

return statement=, 68

return type references, 158-159

return types, 158-159

returning references to objects, 201

returning values, 372-374

right-shift operator (>>) (istream class), 251

routines
   conversion, 210
   I/O, 42
   RTL (runtime library), 4
   startupcode, 4

RTL(RunTime Library), 4, 107, 437

RTTI (Runtime Type Information), 401
   compiler settings, 408-409
   conflicts with virtual functions, 410

_ _rtti modifier, 409

Run command (Debug menu), 7, 10

Runtime Library functions, 37

runtime nodes (project window), 34

S

Save command (File menu), 6

_ _saveregs modifier, 136

scanf function, 47-48

scope of classes, 189

scope of variables, 69-81

scope operator (::), 187

scope resolution, 240-241

T

U

V

W

X–Y–Z